PARENTING IN A CULTURE WAR

Saving the World by Saving Your Family

Zachary C Terry

Maximum Life, Inc.

CONTENTS

PARENTING IN A CULTURE WAR

Saving The World By Saving Your Family

INTRODUCTION

A NOTE TO PARENTS

I live on a barrier Island off the coast of Florida. Many years ago, pirates frequented our little harbor and wreaked havoc up and down the coast of the Americas. These pirates would ruthlessly assault and pillage civilian vessels, sinking them if they could not retool them for their own nefarious purposes.

In the same way, ideological pirates have commandeered the ship of culture with our kids on board. Society is now sailing in a whole new direction. I propose we take back the ship.

Make no mistake, this will not be easy. The pirates have us outnumbered. They have the momentum in their favor. They have already successfully shackled (*canceled*) many of our most valiant warriors in the brig.

The plan I propose in this book is not to raise our own Jolly Roger flag but to look to a more ancient battle plan. If we are to turn things around, we must save the world by saving our family.

I am convinced that the most frightening thing on the planet to that old Satanic Black Beard is a Christian family worshipping on the Lord's Day, breaking bread in harmony, having in-depth discussions about truth, and then showing hospitality to the world around them until a mutiny occurs. It has happened before, many times, and it can happen again.

So, let's batten down the hatches, swab the decks, and wage war on Black Beard. Savvy?

CHAPTER ONE

RELEASING OUR ARROWS

How to Parent Well Amidst a Culture War

Do you feel the pressure?

> *American Christian ideals and values have shifted in alarming ways and your kids are growing up in a dramatically different culture than any generation before them. The moral foundations of society are being shaken and there's no telling what's next.*

Rest assured, if you find yourself concerned about what the future holds for your kids and this generation, you're not alone. As history reveals, rarely does one generation surpass their predecessors morally or spiritually.

I've even heard it said, *"The compromises of one generation become the excesses of the next."*

Think about it: David had Bathsheba, Solomon had many Bathshebas. One generation sows the wind; the next reaps the hurricane. At this point, it seems the only thing standing between the next generation and complete disintegration is us—parents.

Speaking specifically to the powerful effect of moms in a society's character, Napoleon once said: *"Let France have great mothers, and France will have great sons!"*

This is why it's so crucial to examine the role of a parent in the culture we find ourselves in today. How can we best prepare our kids for the world they are inheriting? How can we impress upon their hearts a sense of urgency, duty, and obedience to live and lead in a way that honors God?

First, remind yourself that perhaps you are here, in the words of Mordecai from the book of Esther, "for such a time as this" (Esther 4:14).

Some things in life we choose; others are chosen for us. You didn't choose the family you were born into. You didn't choose the color of your skin or your specific ethnicity. Nor did you choose where you were born. And certainly, you didn't choose to live in this period of time, dealing with the battles raging around us as believers in Christ.

Think of it… would you have chosen to raise your kids in today's society?

Probably not, but the fact is you were chosen to raise your kids in this society. And that means you have a God-given role to play in shaping them into all He created them to be and do in this specific cultural moment. The question is how?

Let God Lead!

In Psalm 127, Solomon characterizes the parent as a warrior on active duty. The weapons at your disposal are not bombs and missiles, but rather children. Let's dive into this psalm and look at the four pictures he paints for us:

> [1] Unless the Lord builds the house, those who build it labor in vain.

The first picture could be described as a construction crew. The idea is that workers are building a house, but in actuality, the Lord is building it through them. Here we see the two opposite approaches to home building: Building with the Lord and building without the Lord. *Are you depending on the Holy Spirit for guidance, wisdom, and strength as you build your home?* Solomon is telling us that we can raise the frame and stack the bricks, but it is a complete waste of time without the Lord overseeing the project.

Next, he utilizes the picture of a watchman…

> [1b] Unless the Lord watches over the city, the watchman stays awake in vain.

During the time in which Solomon is writing, the most advantageous hours to besiege a city were at night while the men were sleeping. A wise king would set watchmen on the walls of the city and when they saw a threat coming from afar, they would awaken the warriors to defend the city. Here we see that the Lord must *also* watch over the city, or the watchmen are pretty much useless! *Are you asking God to protect your family and guard you against the enemy? Are you trusting him to do it?*

Next comes the laborer…

> [2] It is in vain that you rise up early and go late to rest, eating the bread of anxious toil; for he gives to his beloved sleep.

This verse describes your number one employee. She has read all the books in the productivity section and has a highly regimented approach to her day. She gets up before her competition and works later than anyone else. And she not only works hard; she works smart. But here again, the psalmist says that her work will never meet the deepest needs of her soul. *Are you trying to do it all? Or worse, are you trying to control it all? You were never meant to.*

Finally, Solomon gives us the answer we're searching for and hints that there is a better way. This approach will give you sleep at night as well as deep meaning and fulfillment. Take a look at verses 3–5:

> [3] Behold, children are a heritage from the Lord, the fruit of the womb a reward. [4] Like arrows in the hand of a warrior are the children of one's youth. [5] Blessed is the

> man who fills his quiver with them! He shall not be put
> to shame when he speaks with his enemies in the gate.

What is the psalmist's answer to a meaningless life? A man and a woman joined in marriage bringing new life into the world. Those children, he says, are like arrows in the hands of skilled warriors. They are produced, polished, pointed, and propelled into the enemy front lines.

Now, this is not to say that the only meaningful marriages are those that produce children. In fact, a careful study of history will reveal that many of the greatest leaders had no male descendants to carry on their family name… George Washington, the apostle Paul, and Jesus Christ Himself to name a few! History is packed full of people who made a significant difference in the world but did not have biological children.

But if we are going to raise our kids as arrows in this culture war, we must better understand our enemy. Let's look at a few of the strategies he is using today in an effort to keep us all ineffective.

Three Weapons the Enemy Wields Against this Generation

Make no mistake, the enemy has a battle plan to come against your kids on three specific fronts.

The first weapon Satan uses is called androgyny. This is when an individual expresses both masculine and feminine characteristics, whether physically or emotionally. The temptation here is to dress all your kids in beige and eliminate anything distinctly masculine or feminine about them.

This is not the first time Satan has used androgyny to tear apart society. Perhaps there is no better example of the spread of androgyny through a culture than that of seventeenth-century France.

The official portrait of King Louis the 13th portrays him in spiked battle armor with weapons at the ready. By the time his son, King Louis the 14th took the throne things had changed. His official portrait shows him sporting a long feminine wig, stockings, and makeup. This trend was commonplace throughout the Aristocracy of France.

The feminization of men and excesses of the Aristocracy led to the rise of Napoleon in the early eighteenth century, and many of those feminine aristocrats found themselves in the guillotine. Three hundred years later, the guillotine is gone, but androgyny remains.

The second trap set for our kids is known as gnostic theology.

Gnostic thinking emerged in the early centuries of the church as a challenge to biblical teaching on the nature of the physical world. Gnostics denied that Jesus came in the flesh because, in their view, the physical world was irredeemably evil.

Consider 2 John 1:7…

> For many deceivers have gone out into the world, those who do not confess the coming of Jesus Christ in the flesh. Such a one is the deceiver and the antichrist.

The Gnostics believed that the spiritual self was androgynous and could choose whether to express itself as male or female. Hence the idea of a man saying that he feels like a woman trapped in a man's body.[1]

But what does Scripture teach on this matter? Gender cuts deep—all the way to the soul. In fact, in 10 million years, you will have the very same gender that you had at conception. It's true! Your resurrected body will have reproductive organs. To reject your gender is to say that God made a mistake. Can you see the subtle deception?

Your children are born into a world where Bruce Jenner was declared "Woman of the Year" by Glamour magazine. And even more recently, transgender college runner Sadie Schreiner won three women's events at the Liberty League championship meet (Division III). He competed in the men's category a year earlier and placed 19th. And so it is with modern sports. We are all expected to play along with the charade, and further, to champion such confused individuals as cultural heroes.

Thirdly, children today face the lie of perpetual adolescence, a failure to transition into adulthood. Sound familiar? Many kids in this generation are being sent into the world with very little clarity or direction on what it means to be human, to pursue the good, and to live fully. Is there any wonder why young people avoid marriage until later and later in life? When they do get married, they often lack an accurate understanding of the biblical roles of husbands and wives.

In 2016, 15 percent of millennials lived in their parents' home. Fast forward four years, this figure jumped to 52 percent of young adults living with their parents.[2] At times, this can be necessary and even healthy. The danger comes when children rely on their parents well into adulthood to pay the bills and buy the food, while they either make no income or leverage their income for personal pleasure rather than contributing to the needs of the family.

Giving into these cultural pressures will only set our kids up for more failure. So what's the answer? Now that we know what not to do, let's examine three things that may help us get it right.

Accentuate Gender

From the earliest ages, cooperate with God by parenting your kids according to their gender. There are certain cultural trappings that accentuate gender, and they are not all bad. For example, there are certain ways that culture expects a man who embraces his masculinity to dress. A cultural stereotype might see masculinity as playing in the dirt and wrestling, and femininity as playing with baby dolls and having tea parties.

But the biblical framework goes far deeper than cultural stereotypes.

Masculinity, at the principal level, is the glad assumption of sacrificial responsibility. It provides and protects. Masculinity initiates while femininity responds. Femininity in a woman is a virtue while effeminacy in a man is a vice.

Why is it that some Christians in our culture tend to believe there is something un-Christlike about masculinity? Jesus formed cords into a whip and violently drove the money changers out of the 30 acres of property. Many hear that and think, "How un-Christlike!"

We see little boys who are always compliant and gentle; they always keep the rules, they never rock the boat, and we applaud them and tell them they should be a pastor one day. But what about the boy who comes home with a black eye and is regularly sent to the principal's office? Perhaps that kid is simply expressing his God-given masculinity, and he might be just the kind of pastor we need in this generation. After he matures of course!

And as for the biblical framework for girls, they are glorifiers. In 1 Corinthians 11:7, Paul tells us, "… woman is the glory of man." Adam was taken from the ground and he is created for the ground. His job was to serve the ground and make it more fruitful. Eve, on the other hand, was taken from Adam and was created for Adam, as his helper. Just as Adam served the ground and made it better. Eve was to serve Adam and make him better.

Adam gathers the grain, gives it to Eve, and she glorifies it and makes it bread. In the same way, Adam gives his seed to Eve, she glorifies it and gives him a child. A woman has a God-given ability to improve things. Give her a house and she will fashion it into a home.

Julie and I have two daughters and one son. Our son was always utilitarian and pragmatic. When he was old enough to decide what his room should be like, he wanted to ensure he had easy access to all of his stuff. Our daughters, on the other hand, would glorify their rooms. They were concerned about the visual aesthetic, the aroma, even the type of music that would perpetually play lightly in the background. Our girls made their rooms into an oasis of contentment; our son made his room into a fortress of solitude.

That tendency is not a design flaw; it is a design feature. God made them that way. Things work best when we intentionally raise our sons to be providers and protectors and our daughters to be glorifiers.

Celebrate Maturity

Have you ever witnessed a mother treating one of her kids who is older as if they were a toddler? It's one of the most damaging things we can do to our children and their development into maturity.

God gave your child to you as a baby, you should enjoy that fully! Coddle them, care for them, and nurture them to your heart's content. But as your child transitions into new stages of development, so should the way you treat them.

Just as it is not right for you to reject their God-given gender, it is equally wrong for you to reject their God-given maturity. In other words, God designed them to grow into adults... *so let them do it!*

The best way to do this is by establishing ceremonies that celebrate rites of passage. Be intentional about celebrating each new season of development in your child's life and make clear what will change for them in responsibilities and expectations.

The following list contains seven clear stages of maturity, each of which should be celebrated...

1. Infant to toddler: When a child is able to walk on her own, it's time for her to pick up her own toys! Babies cry and

throw a tantrum, but toddlers can use words, so tantrums are no longer acceptable.

2. Toddler to grade school: It's now time to socialize your child and teach him how to get along with others. He will learn to get dressed and be on time during this phase.

3. Grade school to Junior High: Your child is now responsible enough to wake up on their own, get ready for school, and prepare their own breakfast/lunch. Maybe they catch the bus and perhaps they engage in team sports. It's also time for them to take responsibility for their own faith journey.

4. Junior High to High School: Your child is now responsible for a vehicle. She should now be expected to contribute financially to the welfare of the home, which may include getting (and keeping) a job. Allow her to buy her own clothes on occasion, and make sure she has age-appropriate chores around the house.

5. High school to College: Now your child is responsible for living apart from mom and dad, and possibly even paying for their own car insurance. I suggest taking care of your college student's housing and health insurance but leaving the rest to them.

6. College to Single Adult: If your child lives at home, they should be expected to contribute by paying rent or covering a portion of the utilities.

7. Adult to New Family: At this point, children are entirely on their own. The relationship between the parents and the child has transitioned from one of caretaker in varying degrees to the role of sage. You are now a source of godly wisdom as they raise their own family.

Demonstrate Marriage

I believe that 90 percent of what your kids need to know in order to be successful amid a culture war can be learned by observing a healthy marriage relationship.

Dad, you demonstrate masculinity by providing for your family, protecting them, and making them feel safe. You demonstrate leadership by going first in areas of spirituality and faith. You demonstrate maturity by navigating the challenges of life, by not blame-shifting, and by showing them how you willingly submit to authorities in your life. You show them how a husband is to love and care for his wife above all other earthly relationships.

Mom, you demonstrate femininity by loving, supporting, and following the leadership of your husband. You don't demand your kids obey you while constantly bucking against the leadership of your husband. You show them how a godly woman glorifies things. You demonstrate maturity by growing in emotional stability and practicing your spiritual disciplines.

Sounds pretty old-fashioned, right?

That's okay. Consider these words adapted from Bobbie Pingaro's 1967 article in *Guideposts Magazine* titled "The Meanest Mother in the World"…

> *Was your mom a mean, old-fashioned mom? Ours was. While other kids ate candy for breakfast, we had to have cereal, eggs, and toast. While others had a Pepsi and a Twinkie for lunch, we had to eat sandwiches. As you can guess, our mother fixed us a dinner that was different from what other kids had, too.*
>
> *Mother insisted on knowing where we were at all times. You would think we were convicts in a prison. She had to know who our friends were and what we were doing with them.*

She insisted that if we said we would be gone for an hour that we would be gone for an hour or less.

We were ashamed to admit it, but she had the nerve to break the child labor laws by making us work. We had to wash the dishes, make the beds, learn to cook, vacuum the floor, do laundry, empty the trash, and do all sorts of cruel jobs. I think she would lie awake at night thinking of more things for us to do. She always insisted on us telling the truth, the whole truth, and nothing but the truth.

By the time we were teenagers, she could read our minds. Then life got really tough. Mother wouldn't let our friends just honk the horn when they drove up. They had to come up to the door so she could meet them. While everyone else could date when they were 12 or 13, we had to wait until we were 16.

Because of our mother, we missed out on lots of things that other kids experienced. None of us have been caught shoplifting, vandalizing other's property, or ever arrested for any crime. It was all her fault.

Now that we have left home, we are all educated, honest adults. And to tell you the truth, we are doing our best to be mean, old-fashioned parents like Mom…

Give your kids the boundaries they need to lead healthy, productive, God-honoring lives. When it's hard (and it will get hard), remember the truth of Hebrews 12:11…

For the moment all discipline seems painful rather than pleasant, but later it yields the peaceful fruit of righteousness to those who have been trained by it.

Resist the urge to make your child happy in the moment and instead do what is best for them in the long run. See the big picture and parent with the end in mind. Only then will you experience the fruit of verses 12 and 13…

12 Therefore lift your drooping hands and strengthen your weak knees, **13** and make straight paths for your feet, so that what is lame may not be put out of joint but rather be healed.

Yes, we're in a culture war. And yes, we need energy and endurance for this parenting marathon. Walk in confidence with the truth of God's Word lighting the way, trusting in Him alone to make your paths straight.

Questions to Consider:

1. When you ponder the culture in which you are raising your kids, what concerns you the most? What feels most urgent to you as you fight these battles?

2. In what ways have you been tempted to clear a path for your kids, making sure they avoid all obstacles? Do you feel this has hindered their maturity? Why is it important to allow our kids to be uncomfortable or experience hardship? What can we do to support them in those times?

3. How can you and your spouse do a better job of modeling a Christ-like marriage to your kids? What habits or attitudes need to be adjusted?

4. What is one tangible way you can release your kids to God's care and remember each day that it's His strength you need?

CHAPTER TWO

THE THREAT OF CULTURAL MARXISM

"Why is Everyone Clapping?"

Aleksandr Solzhenitsyn writes in his book, *The Gulag Archipelago* of a speech given in 1937 by Soviet leader Joseph Stalin. If you've heard clips of Stalin, you know that he was not a moving orator, but he didn't have to be. He had the power of the totalitarian state behind him. When this particular speech concluded, a thunderous applause resonated across the hall for six… seven… eight minutes. Can you imagine?

After 11 minutes of clapping, the director of the local paper mill who was in attendance decided that it had been enough, and he politely sat down. Later that same night, the director was arrested and sent to prison for ten years. The authorities cited an "official" reason for his sentence but during his interrogation, he was told, *"Don't ever be the first to stop clapping."*

George Lucas captured the sentiment well in his Star Wars Prequel with the statement, *"How does freedom die? To thunderous applause."*

Things are happening in our country today that cause those of us with a Christian worldview to ask, *"Why is everyone clapping?"* The Bible offers insight into the importance of cultural understanding when we read about the future King David. After God rejected Saul as king, He sought a man after His own heart and found such a man in the shepherd boy David, son of Jessie the Bethlehemite.

Samuel anointed David as king and Saul spent the next fifteen years furiously trying to retain power, despite the hand of God compelling him away from the throne. In 1 Chronicles 12, God sends David the men he will need to successfully establish himself as king in Israel. He provides ambidextrous bowmen, experienced warriors, and perhaps most importantly, men who had an *"understanding of the times."* Only then would Israel know what to do. In the same way, it's crucial for us as believers in Christ to understand *our* times in order to respond biblically.

America: A Christian Nation?

I'm often asked, *"Is America a Christian nation?"* In one sense, no nation can be fully Christian because Christ died for individual people, not geo-political entities. People, and only people, can be Christians according to the essential meaning of the word. There can, however, be a Christian consensus within a nation. Few would disagree that the founding fathers of this nation shared a Christian consensus. Men like George Washington, John Adams, and Samuel Adams were devout Christians, and others like Thomas Jefferson and Benjamin Franklin (although more deist than theologically orthodox Christians) shared a Judeo-Christian worldview that shaped their understanding. Out of this Christian consensus, these men drafted our Declaration of Independence, our Constitution, and our Bill of Rights—the documents that formed and have guided our nation since its founding.

Consider the threats our nation has faced since her inception:

- The British monarchy, who wished to keep the country as part of its colonial empire, was met with the unshakeable tenacity of early patriots.

- Totalitarian forces of Nazi Germany and Imperial Japan were defeated by the sheer might and technological advancements of American ingenuity.

- Soviet Russia collapsed as America's optimism was stirred to new heights under the leadership of Ronald Reagan.

- The subversive terrorism of Al-Qaeda and Osama Bin Laden was answered with the unified voice and fist of our military as we counterpunched with all our might.

- And most recently, the biological threat of COVID-19 resulted in our brightest minds working endlessly to meet this new and peculiar challenge.

Each one of these threats drew blood and posed great dangers, yet each was soundly defeated. There is, however, one threat that has taken a much more subtle approach. Sadly, it is finding great success to *thunderous applause.* This threat did not come in the form of a missile or a contagion, it came in the form of *ideas.* These ideas are like seeds planted in young minds, generation after generation, until the Christian consensus on which we were founded seems so fragile that one wonders if it can support the weight of the republic.

What threat am I referring to? The threat of cultural Marxism.

Not only did German born Karl Marx not share America's Christian consensus, but he despised it. In fact, some have even described him as possessed by a demon or a friend of the devil. Marx's partner, Friedrich Engels, declared that ten thousand devils had Marx by the hair. In 2020, Paul Kengor wrote a book titled *The Devil and Karl Marx.* According to Kengor, Marx was a tyrant, a racist, and a misogynistic radical who hated God and wanted to see the world burn. In his 1837 poem "The Pale Maiden," Marx composed these self-descriptive words: "*Thus heaven I've forfeited, I know it full well. My soul, once true to God, is chosen now for hell.*"[3]

In 1852, after sowing his godless ideology across Europe, Marx began to write for the New York Daily Tribune. America at that time did not serve as good soil for Marxism. Why? Because the Christian consensus was still thriving. This ideology did however take root in universities of revolutionary Russia. A young student Vladimir Lenin became a follower of Marx after reading, *Das Kapital* in 1867. Lenin rose to power amidst the chaos of the revolution, followed by his protege, also well versed in the principles of Marxist ideology, Joseph Stalin. By this time, Russia shared a Marxist consensus in the same way that America held a Christian consensus.

The seeds of Marxist thought began to take root in universities of the United States, Columbia University in particular, as the Christian consensus began to crumble. By the year 2000, enough young people had a favorable view of Marxism that democratic socialist Bernie Sanders made a strong run for the presidency.

Nevertheless, true economic Marxism can only be instituted in the chaos of revolution. Marx predicted a violent worker's revolt in America that never took place. As a result, a change in strategy was required to spread Marxist ideology in America.

Considering the prevailing Christian consensus that existed in America, Marxism could not spread through the barrel of a gun pointed at the halls of power. This new form of Marxism would spread like a contagion, infecting the structural units of society, especially the family.

Critical Race Theory and Intersectionality

Economic Marxism can be defined this way: *From each according to his ability, to each according to his need.* Marxism in this sense is diametrically opposed to capitalism. It finds its ultimate expression in a socialist or communistic system. Cultural Marxism, on the other hand, leads to an overthrow of cultural norms.

What America has witnessed in the last five to ten years can be described as a tsunami of cultural Marxist ideas that are changing the landscape of our country, and in the process, leading young people into an atheistic, anti-Christian, socialistic worldview. So what ideas are we talking about? Two examples of Marxist thinking include Critical Race Theory (CRT) and intersectionality. CRT argues that the hegemony (*that is the dominant leadership structure*) has influenced the norms of culture in a way that oppresses anyone outside the hegemony. The supposed cultural hegemony in our country is as follows: patriarchal, white, male, heterosexual, cisgendered (*meaning that your identity correlates with your biological gender*), Christian, able-bodied, native-born Americans.

If that describes you, you are the hegemony... and according to cultural Marxism, you have had inordinate influence over culture and thus designed culture to oppress minorities. Who are minorities? Anyone who is not in the hegemony. Thus, women (*who make up at least 50 percent of the population*) are considered a minority group, simply because they are not in the hegemony.

Cultural Marxism suggests that by nature of being a white, male, heterosexual, cisgendered, Christian, able-bodied, native-born American, one is automatically privileged and even racist by virtue of the hegemony. For everyone not in the hegemony, your level of marginalization and oppression stems from the number of areas in which you don't align with the hegemony (*e.g., race, religion, gender*). This is referred to as intersectionality. And these are the principles being taught at the university level as undisputed facts. Even some of today's churches have jumped on the bandwagon as pastors are calling their congregations to repent of certain sins that they never actually committed.

Victor Davis Hanson is the Martin and Illie Anderson Senior Fellow in Residence in Classics and Military History at the Hoover Institution at Stanford University, and professor emeritus of Classics at California State University, Fresno. He is a leader in a secular university and wrote an op-ed for the *Las Vegas Review Journal* where he raised the question, "*Are Americans Being Sovietized?*"[4] In other words, is there an organized plan to spread Marxist propaganda in the U.S., similar to what took place following the Russian Revolution?

Hanson goes on to highlight ten similarities between the spread of Marxist thought in Soviet Russia and the spread of the same in modern day America:

1. In Soviet Russia, there was no escape from ideological indoctrination. Whether you were at home, at work, at a movie, or at a sporting event, it was present. Everything in the culture was leveraged to indoctrinate. And today in America, this even includes certain churches.

2. The press worked with the party and was no longer independent. *Pravda*, or "truth," was the official megaphone of the state, as it simply parroted the talking points provided by the administration.

3. Surveillance was used to ferret out ideological dissidents. Recently, we learned that the U.S. Postal Service admitted to using tracking programs to monitor the social media postings of Americans.

4. The Soviet educational system sought not to enlighten but to indoctrinate young minds in proper government-approved thought.

5. The Soviet Union was run by a pampered elite, exempt from the ramifications of their own radical ideologies. Now in America, Silicon Valley billionaires casually propagate socialism while living in luxury.

6. The Soviets mastered Trotskyism (named after Russian revolutionary leader Leon Trotsky), the rewriting of history, to fabricate a present reality. Are Americans

any different when they indulge in a frenzy of name-changing, statue-toppling, monument-defacing, book-banning, and cancel-culturing?

7. The Soviets created a climate of fear and rewarded stool pigeons for rooting out all potential enemies of the people. Here in the U.S., systems are being designed to turn citizens against one another. Overhear an ill-considered word in a private conversation and you can now destroy a person's career in the court of public opinion.

8. Soviet courts were weaponized according to Marxist ideology.
Today in America, burglars, rioters, and violent offenders in politically correct sanctuary cities defy the law with impunity, knowing the courts will not prosecute them. Jury members are terrified of being doxed and hunted down for an unfavorable verdict.

9. The Soviets doled out prizes based solely on ideological alignment. In modern America, the Pulitzer Prizes, Emmys, Grammys, Tonys, and Oscars don't necessarily reflect the year's best work, but often the most politically correct work from the most woke artists.

10. The Soviets offered no apologies for extinguishing freedom. Instead, they boasted that they were advocates for equity, champions of the underclass, and enemies of privilege. Meanwhile, millions were imprisoned, starved, or murdered.

These are the times in which we live. And make no mistake, this agenda is spreading to the sound of thunderous applause.

Withstanding Cultural Pressure

In Daniel chapter 3, we read of a similar cultural conflict. The Hebrews were born into a nation that was under God's judgement. Babylon had invaded the southern kingdom of Judah, and as was their habit, they had taken the best and brightest captives back to the capital to recondition them into a Babylonian worldview. Key among the indoctrination was a statue mentioned in verse 1:

Daniel 3:1…

> [1] King Nebuchadnezzar made an image of gold, whose height was sixty cubits and its breadth six cubits. He set it up on the plain of Dura, in the province of Babylon.

Nebuchadnezzar instructed that when the cacophony of instruments began to play, everyone was to fall to the ground and worship the statue. But then Babylonian officials noticed that some were not bowing, and they complained to the king…

> [12] "There are certain Jews whom you have appointed over the affairs of the province of Babylon: Shadrach, Meshach, and Abednego. These men, O king, pay no attention to you; they do not serve your gods or worship the golden image that you have set up." [13] Then Nebuchadnezzar in furious rage commanded that Shadrach, Meshach, and Abednego be brought. So they brought these men before the king. [14] Nebuchadnezzar answered and said to them, "Is it true, O Shadrach, Meshach, and Abednego, that you do not serve my gods or worship the golden image that I have set up? [15] Now if you are ready when you hear the sound of the horn, pipe, lyre, trigon, harp, bagpipe, and every kind of music, to fall down and worship the image that I have made, well and good. But if you do not worship, you shall immediately be cast into a burning fiery furnace. And who is the god who will deliver you out of my

hands?"

Talk about cancel culture! If you do not applaud the indoctrination of Babylon, you will be canceled to a crisp. How did these men find the courage and strength to face this level of spiritual opposition? I'd love to share with you four principles from this text that will help you withstand cultural pressure today. It's crucial that we teach these truths to our families in the midst of what is quickly becoming America's own blazing furnace.

First, trust the power of God.

> [16] Shadrach, Meshach, and Abednego answered and said to the king, "O Nebuchadnezzar, we have no need to answer you in this matter. [17] If this be so, our God whom we serve *is able to deliver us* from the burning fiery furnace, and he will deliver us out of your hand, O king."

You see, the battle is not ultimately Democrat against Republican, liberal against conservative, or Jew against Babylonian… it is Satan against God.

Someone once said to me, *"Pastor, I wish you wouldn't talk about abortion, just stay out of politics."* Well, the truth is, I have no desire to step into politics, but when the very lives of those made in the image of God are threatened, politics has now stepped into *my* territory. And at that point, it is in fact a matter of theology. If you do not wish to see the Christian consensus in your family washed away, immerse your kids in everything your Bible-believing church has to offer. Then, when they are faced with the wrath of Babylon, they will know how to stand, trusting in the power of God.

Secondly, trust the providence of God.

Shadrach, Meshach, and Abednego trusted in God's power to save them, but their allegiance to Him did not depend on their being saved from the fire. They trusted in His will.

> ^{18} "But if not, be it known to you, O king, that we will not serve your gods or worship the golden image that you have set up."

In other words, "*We will not clap!*"

At the start of World War II, as the German soldiers swept across Europe, British forces found themselves forced to retreat to the beaches of Dunkirk, trapped between the sea and certain death. The German Luftwaffe (air force) dropped leaflets from the air telling the 350,000 British soldiers that resistance was futile —they must either surrender or die. In response to their dire situation, the British commander telegrammed back to England three simple words to communicate their plan: "*But... if... not...*" You see, at that time, Great Britain shared a Christian consensus and the commander knew that his countrymen back home would immediately associate his telegram with this scene in Daniel chapter 3. The point is this: God is not required to vindicate us if and when we stand for truth.

Hebrews 11 unpacks for us that great "hall of faith" with the names of those who overcame and were victorious. Consider these verses from Hebrews 11:32–38:

> ^{32} And what more shall I say? For time would fail me to tell of Gideon, Barak, Samson, Jephthah, of David and Samuel and the prophets— ^{33} who through faith conquered kingdoms, enforced justice, obtained promises, stopped the mouths of lions...

Sometimes it happens that way, God allows you to bring Him glory by winning! But not always...

> ^{36} Others suffered mocking and flogging, and even chains and imprisonment. ^{37} They were stoned, they were sawn in two, they were killed with the sword. They went about in skins of sheep and goats, destitute, afflicted, mistreated— ^{38} of whom the world was not

worthy—wandering about in deserts and mountains, and in dens and caves of the earth.

Sometimes you glorify God by losing. And then there are the words of Jesus from Matthew 5:11–12:

> [11] "Blessed are you when others revile you and persecute you and utter all kinds of evil against you falsely on my account. [12] Rejoice and be glad, for your reward is great in heaven, for so they persecuted the prophets who were before you."

Sometimes, God calms the storm, and other times, He calms you in the midst of the storm. This leads to the third principle, you need to stand for Christ in the face of cultural pressure.

Third, trust the presence of God.

> [24] Then King Nebuchadnezzar was astonished and rose up in haste. He declared to his counselors, "Did we not cast three men bound into the fire?" They answered and said to the king, "True, O king." [25] He answered and said, "But I see four men unbound, walking in the midst of the fire, and they are not hurt; and the appearance of the fourth is like a son of the gods." (Daniel 3:24–25)

Right there, in the midst of the fire, the pre-incarnate Jesus Christ steps into the scene. *You are never closer to Jesus than when you are suffering for his sake.* Remember the words Saul heard on the road to Damascus? *"Saul, Saul, why are you persecuting me?"* He responded, *"Who are you?"* (Acts 22:7). In other words, I don't even know you! How can I persecute you? Jesus tells us in the Gospels that He identifies with His people in their suffering. He says, *"To persecute them is to persecute me."*

You will never suffer alone, the One who suffered for you on the cross promises to hold you as you carry your own cross for Him. And not only will God be present with you, in His own way and timing, He will also vindicate your faith.

Fourth, trust the promotion of God.

> [28] Nebuchadnezzar answered and said, "Blessed be the God of Shadrach, Meshach, and Abednego, who has sent his angel and delivered his servants, who trusted in him, and set aside the king's command, and yielded up their bodies rather than serve and worship any god except their own God. [29] Therefore I make a decree: Any people, nation, or language that speaks anything against the God of Shadrach, Meshach, and Abednego shall be torn limb from limb, and their houses laid in ruins, for there is no other god who is able to rescue in this way." [30] Then the king promoted Shadrach, Meshach, and Abednego in the province of Babylon.

God not only delivered these faithful warriors, He elevated them, vindicating their faith. It was their refusal to clap that ultimately gave credence to their faith. There is something about taking a stand that lends credibility to your faith claims.

Pastor and Bible scholar Dr. Henry Blackaby once said, *"Do you not already hear the warnings of God? Do you not see that the enemy is coming in like a flood? God is trying to raise up a standard against it and you and I are that standard."*[5]

You can always trust in God's power, providence, and presence when you stand for Him—and you can be certain that He will honor your courage by promoting your faith as a testimony to who He is.

So take a stand and refuse to let your freedom die to a thunderous applause.

Questions to consider:

1. Do you believe there is still a "Christian consensus" in America? Why or why not? Can you think of a recent example in which you have personally experienced a

shift in cultural norms?

2. From the article *"Are Americans Being Sovietized?"*, which of the ten similarities between Marxist thought in Soviet Russia and what we are seeing today in America concerns you the most?

3. Like Daniel, we face many cultural pressures today and it seems as though they are only intensifying. In what specific ways have you experienced cultural pressure as a believer in Christ? How can you practically trust God in such situations? What Scriptures might help?

CHAPTER THREE

THE CHRISTIAN'S RESPONSE TO CULTURAL MARXISM

Important Steps Toward Rebuilding American Values

In light of the threat of cultural Marxism and the movements that have come from these ideas, I'd like to suggest that what we are experiencing in America is not incidental. It's organized, intentional, and your home is in the crossfire. In *1984*, George Orwell's scathing novel denouncing the horrors of totalitarian control, he writes,

> *"He who controls the past, controls the future. He who controls the present controls the past."* [6]

Now that Marxism has attained such influence in media, higher education, and even some churches, we are beginning to see a rewriting of both biblical and American history. In the midst of this cultural quagmire led by well-trained, determined advocates, churches, and pastors are refusing to speak up. Even worse, they are getting on board the train to destruction. I am reminded of the poem by William Butler Yeats entitled, "The Second Coming"...

> Turning and turning in the widening gyre
> The falcon cannot hear the falconer;
> Things fall apart; the centre cannot hold;
> Mere anarchy is loosed upon the world,

> The blood-dimmed tide is loosed, and everywhere
> The ceremony of innocence is drowned;
> *The best lack all conviction, while the worst*
> *Are full of passionate intensity.*[7]

Yeats' grim scene eerily reflects the world we live in today. But ours is not the first moment in history to know this kind of upheaval. The nation of Israel under the leadership of Nehemiah faced a similar challenge. Fresh off their return from exile in Babylon, Israel had momentum, was moving in a good direction, and the walls of the city were being reestablished. Then suddenly, the enemy attacked. Sanballat, Tobiah, and Geshem were regional governors from among the Horonites and the Ammonites, two groups of people God drove out of the promised land before the Jews entered. They hated the fact that Nehemiah was well on his way to helping the nation of Israel return to its former glory. In fact, these men had a long-standing hatred for Israel.

Read their response in Nehemiah 2:10 after learning that the walls would be rebuilt...

> [10] But when Sanballat the Horonite and Tobiah the Ammonite servant heard this, it displeased them greatly that someone had come to seek the welfare of the people of Israel.

Then in verse 19, Nehemiah records:

> [19] But when Sanballat the Horonite and Tobiah the Ammonite servant and Geshem the Arab heard of it, they jeered at us and despised us and said, "What is this thing that you are doing? Are you rebelling against the king?"

Establishing Strategic Alliances

As Nehemiah's efforts came under attack, he responded in three specific ways that Christians must learn to apply today. First, he established strategic alliances.

Nehemiah 8:1–3 says...

> [1] And all the people gathered as one man into the square before the Water Gate. And they told Ezra the scribe to bring the Book of the Law of Moses that the Lord had commanded Israel. [2] So Ezra the priest brought the Law before the assembly, both men and women and all who could understand what they heard, on the first day of the seventh month. [3]And he read from it facing the square before the Water Gate from early morning until midday, in the presence of the men and the women and those who could understand.

That's over six hours of teaching! Notice that for the political leader Nehemiah to truly rebuild and reform Jerusalem, he had to partner with Ezra, the religious leader. Nehemiah demands the construction of a massive tower built for a man to stand upon and teach... but to everyone's surprise, Nehemiah doesn't teach; Ezra the priest does.

How does this relate to our predicament in America today? If we are going to turn this country around, the church must be engaged in the political process.

French historian Alexis de Tocqueville coined the term American exceptionalism in his 1835 book *Democracy in America*. He points out that America is the exception and not the rule among the nations of the world.

Why is that? Typically, we point to political leaders such as George Washington, John Hancock, and Thomas Jefferson, and certainly they deserve credit for their passion and vision, but in fact, America's spiritual leaders played a major role in paving the way to revolution and the fight for freedom. In an 1816 letter to a young man named Hezekiah Niles, John Adams shared what principles and convictions inspired the American Revolution, as well as which men helped spark the mood of the time. Adams highlights four names in particular that he believed helped lay the foundation for the revolution long before shots were fired. Every one of them was a "reverend." These men preached truth for their time from the pulpit, and it was this partnership between politicians and preachers that set the stage for cultural and political change.

The same proved true for ancient Israel. Look at Nehemiah 8, verses 7–8...

> [7] Also Jeshua, Bani, Sherebiah, Jamin, Akkub, Shabbethai, Hodiah, Maaseiah, Kelita, Azariah, Jozabad, Hanan, Pelaiah, the Levites, helped the people to understand the Law, while the people remained in their places. [8] They read from the book, from the Law of God, clearly, and they gave the sense, so that the people understood the reading.

Sounds like church small groups to me! Change comes about when like-minded people cooperate together toward a common goal. But not only did Nehemiah establish a strategic alliance, he led the way by celebrating.

Intentional Celebration

> [9] And Nehemiah, who was the governor, and Ezra the priest and scribe, and the Levites who taught the people said to all the people, "This day is holy to the Lord your God; do not mourn or weep." For all the people wept as they heard the words of the Law. [10] Then he said to them, "Go your way. Eat the fat and drink sweet wine and send portions to anyone who has nothing ready, for this day is holy to our Lord. And do not be grieved, *for the joy of the Lord is your strength.*"

That last phrase in verse 10 is often quoted, but did you know that it is actually a verse of reproof to people who are crying when they should be laughing and celebrating? It was the evangelist Vance

Havner who said, *"You can't be optimistic with a misty optic."*[8] If we are going to see a better future for America, we must learn to celebrate the goodness of God. Of course, there is plenty going on in the lives of our families, churches, and certainly in the news to keep our spirits low. But instead of feeling defeated, what if we learned to upset the devil by rejoicing in the Lord in the midst of it all? I think incredible things would happen.

As the story continues to unfold in Nehemiah, we see clearly how leaders are thermostats, not thermometers…

> [11] So the Levites calmed all the people, saying, "Be quiet, for this day is holy; do not be grieved."

Did you catch that? The Levites were equating holiness with happiness. And as a leader, one of the key aspects of culture building is knowing what to celebrate and how to celebrate. Believe it or not, I've been criticized in the past for doing a special "patriot service" at our church, and also for the fact that we have an American flag in our auditorium. Why is that important to me? Very simply because I look at this congregation the way I look at my family. It is a parent's job to weave traditions into the life of the family in order to affect the direction. Andy Stanley said it this way, *"What gets celebrated gets repeated."* [9]

There is a reason why the nation of Israel held six different feasts of rejoicing, but only one day of mourning. Clearly, the people of Israel followed Nehemiah's lead…

> [12] And all the people went their way to eat and drink and to send portions and to make great rejoicing, because they had understood the words that were declared to them.

Nothing declares your faith in the gospel better than your ability to celebrate and rejoice. In fact, I find it interesting that the first miracle Jesus ever performed was at a wedding party. And it's even more interesting to me that Jesus and His disciples were even invited! Jesus was asked to hang out with tax collectors and sinners all the time. Could it be because He knew how to celebrate?

Joy is serious business to God. And if believers are going to win people over to our vision for this country, we'll catch more flies with honey than vinegar.

So remember, you are not just a member of a nation under attack, you are a citizen of a city whose builder and maker is God Almighty. Because of that, there is always hope. Teach your family to celebrate what's good and right about America.

Storytelling

Not only did Nehemiah establish strategic alliances and lead the way in intentional celebration, he knew the power of storytelling.

> [14] And they found it written in the Law that the Lord had commanded by Moses that the people of Israel should dwell in booths during the feast of the seventh month, [15] and that they should proclaim it and publish it in all their towns and in Jerusalem, "Go out to the hills and bring branches of olive, wild olive, myrtle, palm, and other leafy trees to make booths, as it is written." [16] So the people went out and brought them and made booths for themselves, each on his roof, and in their courts and in the courts of the house of God, and in the square at the Water Gate and in the square at the Gate of Ephraim. [17] And all the assembly of those who had returned from the captivity made booths and lived in the booths, for from the days of Jeshua the son of Nun to that day the people of Israel had not done so. And there was very great rejoicing.

The booths in this passage were tents, similar to what the Israelites lived in during their forty years in the wilderness.

But don't miss this: All throughout Nehemiah chapter 9, the Levites retell the story of who they are as a people. They tell of the unfolding of creation, the call of Abram, the Exodus, and the giving of the Law. Here in our day, the stories we tell reveal and reinforce the culture we are seeking to establish. Stories unite us around a common narrative as we see ourselves as a part of that story. The sad truth is the reason it is so easy for Marxist thought leaders to rewrite history is because we have often done a poor job of telling our story.

One of the greatest contributions to this world coming out of the Protestant Reformation was a return to the founding documents. You see, Christianity had veered in so many different directions, so much so that no one knew which road to take. That is, until men like Martin Luther taught concepts like *Sola Scriptura*, meaning, "Scripture alone." This concept affirmed that Scripture was the supreme authority on Christian faith and practice. Other authorities such as reason or the church bore weight, but everything submitted to the revealed truth of Scripture. If our nation is going to survive and thrive, we must get back to our founding documents, read them, study them, and hold our leaders accountable to them. We must get back to the Bible.

For those who fought for this country, it can be a hard thing to talk about. But we need to hear you talk about it! Remember what George Orwell said? *"He who controls the past, controls the future."* Tell your story! Tell your children and grandchildren how you came to faith in Jesus. Be inspired by Katherine Hankey who wrote the famous hymn "I Love to Tell the Story" while bedridden…

> *I love to tell the story,*
> *Twill be my theme in glory*
> *To tell the old, old story*
> *Of Jesus and his love!*

Tell your story to someone today. Hope is not lost and neither is the future of America. May God stand beside her and guide her like never before, through the night, with the light from above.

Questions to consider:

1. Nehemiah shows us the importance of strategic alliances and spiritual influences. How is your church responding to the ungodliness we see in our culture today? In what ways are you responding on a personal level?

2. Is there a need in your life for more rejoicing? How can you do a better job of celebrating the history and relevance of America with your family and loved ones?

3. When was the last time you told your story of faith? Could it be that your experience might encourage or spur someone on toward a deeper connection with God? Ask God today to place someone on your heart who needs to hear your story.

4. If our desire is that our nation would "get back to the Bible," what are some practical ways we can start today in our own homes and communities making that vision a reality?

CHAPTER FOUR

EMOTIONAL STABILITY IN A THERAPEUTIC CULTURE

Maintaining a Full Tank in the Midst of Battle

I first remember hearing the word "soul" around the first grade. When staying the night at my friend Shane's house, his mom would often come in and tell us to say our prayers. During this season of my life, I didn't pray much, but my friend Shane said the very same prayer each time I was there. We would kneel by the bed, bow our heads and he would say, "*Now I lay me down to sleep, I pray the Lord my soul to keep. And if I die before I wake, I pray the Lord my soul to take.*"

Let's just say this was not the most comforting prayer to me! How horrible! How am I supposed to sleep peacefully after contemplating my own immediate death? And furthermore, what is this about my soul? The Lord is going to take my soul? I would really like for my soul to be left alone!

Since those days, I have learned to place great value on the care of my soul, as well as the souls of others. Did you know that your soul is made up of three things? It consists of your mind, your will, and your emotions. Your soul is unique in that it operates via a physical apparatus: your brain. As such, your soul can be in danger of trauma or sickness just like any other part of your physical body.

When looking at the issues of our day, the experience of depression has become more prevalent than ever before; although, it has been around a long time. Sixteenth-century Christian mystic St. John of the Cross referred to depression as a "Dark Night of the Soul." John Bunyan captured it better when he referred to the experience in his classic work, *Pilgrim's Progress* as the "*slough of despond.*"

There's a reason why the number one prescribed medication in our country is anti-depressants. According to a new study from the American Academy of Pediatrics, the monthly dispensing rate for prescriptions for young adults and teens has increased nearly 64 percent faster since 2020.[10] If you have experienced or are experiencing some form of depression or anxiety, you are not alone. In fact, we can find many examples of people in the Bible who often struggled with depression.

Let's start with King David. Read his words in Psalm 10:1…

> [1] Why, O Lord, do you stand far away? Why do you hide yourself in times of trouble?

And Psalm 13:1–2:

> [1]How long, O Lord? Will you forget me forever? How long will you hide your face from me? [2] How long must I take counsel in my soul and have sorrow in my heart all the day? How long shall my enemy be exalted over me?

Whether it was fleeing from Saul, mourning the death of his son, or facing the consequences of his own sin, David understood what it felt like to be in an emotional state of sorrow and sadness.

Then there's Elijah. After defeating the prophets of Baal, this prophet of God was gripped with fear and prayed under a broom tree in 1 Kings 19:4…

> "It is enough; now, O Lord, take away my life, for I am no better than my fathers."

And let's not forget Jonah! Despaired of life after the repentance of Nineveh, he says in Jonah 4:3…

> "Therefore now, O Lord, please take my life from me, for it is better for me to die than to live."

Remember this question Job asked in Job 3:11?

> "Why did I not die at birth, come out from the womb and expire?"

Then, later in verse 26,

> "I am not at ease, nor am I quiet; I have no rest, but (only) trouble comes."

And consider the weight of the words of Jeremiah in chapter 20, verse 14:

> Cursed be the day on which I was born! The day when my mother bore me, let it not be blessed!

In the book of Ecclesiastes, Solomon says life is utterly meaningless. Even Paul spoke of having *"great sorrow and unceasing anguish in his heart"* in Romans 9:2. But perhaps the most powerful biblical example comes from the life of our Lord Jesus when He is described in Isaiah 53:3 as a *"man of sorrows and acquainted with grief."* Later in Mark 14:34, we hear Him say in the garden on the night of His arrest, *"My soul is very sorrowful, even to death."*

If Jesus had remained in that state, the pain of His soul itself may have killed Him. In fact, this is where His first drop of blood was shed in the form of sweat… due to the anxiety in His heart.

Depression has been around a long time and impacted countless lives. Even Jesus wrestled with it! So let's take a closer look at where depression often originates and how we as believers are called to respond.

The Causes of Depression

According to the Mayo Clinic, there is no *known* cause for depression. Scientists don't fully understand how imbalances in neurotransmitters cause signs and symptoms of depression. It's just not clear whether changes in neurotransmitters are a cause or a result of depression. Now, certain medications can list depression as a common side effect. Also, chronic Illnesses, such as heart disease, stroke, diabetes, cancer, or Alzheimer's disease also put you at higher risk of developing depression. We also know it can be common for mothers to experience depression a few days to weeks after giving birth, and recent studies suggest the father can also experience similar symptoms.

Then of course there are hormonal changes. Women experience depression about twice as much as men, which leads researchers to believe hormonal factors play a role in its development. If you are battling a depression that cannot be linked to a certain life event, it's important to see a medical professional as there may be a physical cause that would respond to chemical help.

In the case of David, however, his depression seemed to have a spiritual and/or mental origin. To start, we find David engaged in some unhealthy thinking in 1 Samuel 27:1…

> Then David said in his heart, "Now I shall perish one day by the hand of Saul…"

We all talk to ourselves, right? It's not a bad thing to do as long as we're careful about what we are saying. Think about it: Samuel told David that he would be king. Abigail, who would become David's wife, affirmed this in 1 Samuel 25:30. But despite all this, David began to speak things over his life that were simply not true. As a result, he became insecure, doubted God, and lost all hope. What you say to yourself matters. Beyond that, what you think of yourself matters even more. Consider the words of Paul in Philippians 4:8 (NASB1995):

[8] Finally, brethren, whatever is true, whatever is honorable, whatever is right, whatever is pure, whatever is lovely, whatever is of good repute, if there is any excellence and if anything worthy of praise, dwell on these things.

Your emotions follow your thinking. So in order to have healthy emotions, you must engage in healthy thinking. Now, when someone is struggling with depression, they may seek help perhaps from a pastor, a therapist, or a medical doctor. The first step in that process is a myriad of questions about the person and what they are experiencing. Why? Because we must have context. There is no other way to get help than to first provide context. *However,* do you know one of the greatest traps of depression? An unhealthy focus on self. Sometimes, not always, the exit door of depression is shifting the focus off yourself and on to others.

Not only did David engage in unhealthy thinking, but he also held on to unguarded emotions. David had recently experienced major wins including defeating Goliath, overcoming the temptation to kill Saul, overcoming the temptation to kill Nabal, and finding a wife. He had also experienced some major losses, such as Saul turning against him in a demonic fit, Saul trying to kill him numerous times, losing the companionship of his very best friend Jonathan, and losing the guidance and protection of Samuel the prophet. If you find yourself experiencing extreme highs or extreme lows, you will find that depression often follows because you've been exhausted by your emotions. Vince Lombardi said it this way: *"Fatigue makes cowards of us all."* This is why Proverbs 4:23 (NASB1995) states,

> Watch over your heart with all diligence, for from it flows the springs of life.

Emotions are like a muscle... they can fatigue. Any emotion experienced on a high level over a long period of time will fatigue the brain and lure it toward depression. This does not mean emotions are wrong; they are part of how God created you to function, but it does mean that we must guard our emotions in a sinful world—because they will often lead us astray.

The Consequences of Depression

During this period of David's life (1 Samuel 27), the Bible does not contain a single recorded prayer from him. It certainly seems that the fog of depression had clouded David's view of God. Remember what had just happened? Samuel had died. He wasn't there to help guide David or correct his thinking. He was isolated. And in a way, the same happens to us. When we fall into the depth of depression, we don't want to pray, and we often steer clear of church or those who are a part of our Christian communities. Sometimes it just feels too hard to engage.

In the life of David, not only did he stop praying, but he was no longer productive. We have no recorded psalms during this period because, just maybe, it felt as though his song was gone. Many of us, too, lack inspiration and motivation during heavy seasons. It feels easier to just go through the motions and put one foot in front of the other. In
1 Samuel 27:2–3 we read:

> [2] So David arose and went over, he and the six hundred men who were with him, to Achish the son of Maoch, king of Gath. [3] And David lived with Achish at Gath...

Do you remember who is from Gath? Goliath of Gath! There is something about depression that can cause a person to move into enemy territory or toward anything that may offer some relief, even if it's destructive. In light of this illustration, where is your Gath? What is that thing that you battle against when you are in your "right" mind, but when you're not thinking clearly, you dive into it for relief? Is it a bottle? Could it be gambling, pornography, food? Is it excessive shopping or perhaps an illicit relationship? It would do us all good to identify our "Gaths" and be mindful of the idols that offer temporary relief with eternal consequences. Because escaping to your Gath doesn't just hurt you... it hurts others and leaves a ripple effect. Just take a look at 1 Samuel 27:3...

> ³ And David lived with Achish at Gath, he and his men, every man with his household, and David with his two wives, Ahinoam of Jezreel, and Abigail of Carmel, Nabal's widow.

So David goes down into Gath and takes a lot of people with him. This reminds me of the old saying, *"Hurting people hurt people."* It was certainly true of David. First Samuel 27:8–9 says:

> ⁸ Now David and his men went up and made raids against the Geshurites, the Girzites, and the Amalekites, for these were the inhabitants of the land from of old, as far as Shur, to the land of Egypt. ⁹ And David would strike the land and would leave neither man nor woman alive, but would take away the sheep, the oxen, the donkeys, the camels, and the garments, and come back to Achish.

David began to hurt people who were not officially his enemies. Anytime someone becomes unusually emotional or unusually angry, pause for a moment and ask yourself, *"What are they going through?"* Hurting people hurt people. The next consequence we see from the life of David is how his words were becoming more and more vague. When reporting back to Achish in 1 Samuel 27:10, he says:

> ¹⁰ When Achish asked, "Where have you made a raid today?" David would say, "Against the Negeb of Judah," or, "Against the Negeb of the Jerahmeelites," or, "Against the Negeb of the Kenites."

Negeb means "low country." He hadn't raided any of those places. Do you ever notice how kids sometimes respond to questions with words like *"fine"*? One-word answers might be acceptable once in a while but don't allow them to become the norm. Get your kids talking! Make the effort to dig a bit deeper and discover what they're thinking. There is nothing you cannot resolve as a family as long as the lines of communication are open.

This brings me to the next consequence of unaddressed depression… family problems. David and his people were living in a town called Ziglag. In Chapter 30, we read where the Amalikites attack David's position at Ziglag while David and the men are out on a raid. They take his entire family captive. First Samuel 30:4 tells us…

> 4 Then David and the people who were with him raised their voices and wept until they had no more strength to weep.

Then in 1 Samuel 30:6…

> 6 And David was greatly distressed, for the people spoke of stoning him, because all the people were bitter in soul, each for his sons and daughters.

I guess you could say David had finally hit rock bottom. He had nowhere else to look but up.

The Cure for Depression

When you find yourself stuck in an emotional rut, it's important to turn your focus from the horizontal plane to the vertical plane. In other words, look up! We see a shift in David's heart in 1 Samuel 30:6B when we read, *"But David strengthened himself in the Lord his God."* You see, David did what so many of us do. Rather than turning to God before anything else at the onset of discouragement, we turn to Him as a last resort. Why do we wait? We know from God's Word that He wants us to call out to Him in times of distress. Psalm 46:1 tells us that *"God is our refuge and strength, a very present help in trouble."* Jesus taught us to say these words when we pray: *"Deliver us from evil…"* Our Father is well aware that there will be times when we need to be pulled out of a pit. He wants us to call on Him for help in any circumstance of life.

In fact, in 1 Samuel 30:7, David tells the priest to bring him the ephod. This was how God's people in the Old Testament heard from God. We didn't see David seeking God's opinion or help before he went to Gath, but he's sure asking for it now! Could it be that you need to hit rock bottom so the only place you can look is up? Could it be that you are in this place today? Maybe it's time to look up, get in your prayer closet, and say, *"Bring me the ephod"*? The prodigal son we read about in Luke 15 hit rock bottom and after he "came to himself" he said, *"I will arise and go to my father!"*

Second Samuel 1 brings a similar turning point in the life of David. Verses 2–4 say,

> [2] And on the third day, behold, a man came from Saul's camp, with his clothes torn and dirt on his head. And when he came to David, he fell to the ground and paid homage. [3] David said to him, "Where do you come from?" And he said to him, "I have escaped from the camp of Israel." [4] And David said to him, "How did it go? Tell me." And he answered, "The people fled from the battle, and also many of the people have fallen and are dead, and Saul and his son Jonathan are also dead."

Now before you think David was jumping for joy, understand that there was something very sad about the death of Saul (and certainly the death of Jonathan). But this was in fact the key to David's future. He could now, finally, take his place on the throne of Israel. How does this relate to you and me? Can you think of someone who gave their life so that you could be free? When you are at your darkest moment, remember Jesus. He wants to give you the hope, joy and freedom that only He can give.

William Cowper, the well-known poet and hymn writer was reminded of God's sovereign hand in the midst of his own depression. One day, he hired a cab to drive him to a bridge in

London where he intended to take his own life. The driver got lost in that day's unusually heavy London fog when he stopped the cab to let Cowper out. It was then that William Cowper discovered he wasn't at the London bridge at all, but rather the front door of his own house.

He had intended to jump. He meant to die. But somehow God, in His mysterious way, caused that driver to get lost and take Cowper straight back to his home. He dismissed the cab, went back to his study, and reflected on Psalm 22:1–2:

> [1] My God, my God, why have you forsaken me? Why are you so far from saving me, from the words of my groaning? [2] O my God, I cry by day, but you do not answer, and by night, but I find no rest.

It was then that he remembered how Jesus cried out to His Father on that dark, painful night in the garden, yet heaven was silent. Why? So that when we cry to heaven, it will never again be silent. Jesus died that Cowper might live. And there on that foggy night, he penned the words to this classic hymn:

> *"God moves in mysterious ways, His wonders to perform. Plants His footsteps in the sea, and rides upon the storm. Ye fearful saints, fresh courage take. The clouds ye so much dread are big with mercy, And shall break with blessings on your head."*[11]

Questions to consider:

1. Has there been a time in your life when your soul was "downcast" and you were inconsolable? When you think about that season, can you point to a physical/chemical issue, unhealthy thinking patterns, or unguarded emotions?

2. In seasons of depression or anxiety, have you found it difficult to pray and/or seek spiritual community? Why do you think that is? What might help?

3. What is your "Gath"? What negative habits do you lean into when feeling emotionally vulnerable or weak? What boundaries can you put in place to keep you from drifting towards those things?

4. How, like David, can we *strengthen ourselves in the Lord* when life feels hard? And how can remembering what Jesus did for us change our perspectives?

CHAPTER FIVE

THE TRICHOTOMY OF HUMAN NATURE

Engaging the Culture through the Roles of Body, Soul, and Spirit

I heard about a North Carolina lawyer who purchased a box of twenty-four very rare and expensive cigars and insured them against, among many other things, fire. Within a month, he had smoked all twenty-four cigars. Sure enough, the lawyer filed a claim against the insurance company, stating that the cigars were lost in a series of small fires.

The insurance company refused to pay, citing the obvious: The man had consumed the cigars in a normal fashion. However, the lawyer sued and won. Delivering the ruling, the judge made clear that he agreed with the insurance company that the claim was frivolous. However, he also agreed with the lawyer that the insurance company insured the cigars against fire without defining the level or degree of the fire and thus they were obligated to pay the claim. Rather than enduring the lengthy and costly appeals process, the insurance company paid the lawyer $15,000 for his "loss" of the twenty-four cigars.

After the lawyer cashed the check, the insurance company then had him arrested on twenty-four counts of arson.

Life is often a series of small fires. And left unchecked, they can lead to a disastrous end. So often when we face tough issues in our society, the battlefield exists in the mind. Understanding the make-up of a human being is crucial to engaging those around you, especially when it comes to issues like cultural Marxism and gender identity. Developing a biblical view of the roles of the body, mind, and soul offers enormous help in addressing the insidious ideas we find in today's culture.

For years, theologians have debated whether man is essentially a "dichotomy" or a "trichotomy." What is the difference? These two words address the question, *"Does a human essentially exist in two parts or three?"* The answer sometimes gets lost in the original languages of Scripture: Hebrew, Greek, and Aramaic. These languages are more akin to romance languages. They have many words and case endings that convey slight changes of nuance. So, they are much better at capturing the emotional essence of the speaker. The English language, on the other hand, is very linear and compartmentalized. We like dictionaries with clear definitions; thus our language is fairly mathematical and straightforward.

When we translate these ancient romantic languages into our linear English, it's like translating Shakespeare into Calculus. The essential meaning of the text is captured perfectly, but the beauty of the text is sometimes compromised. Take for instance the concept of the word "love." In English, we have one word for love, and we use it ad nauseam. *"I love fried chicken. I love the Florida Gators. I love my wife."* The reader is expected to use context in order to interpret what kind of love I'm referring to by these statements. But the ancients didn't trust the listener as much as we do. They used a variety of words and case endings to make certain they correctly conveyed the intended meaning.

For instance, here are their definitions of the different forms of "love":

- Brotherly love – *Philia*
- Divine love – *Agape*
- Romantic love – *Eros*
- Friendship love – *Pragma*

- Family love – *Storge*
- Flirtatious love – *Ero-tor-opia* or *Ludus*

In the biblical text, each of these words are translated into English as the word "love." And when it comes to understanding a person, there is a similar storehouse of words applied, but the translators are not all in agreement as to what the words specifically reference. Are these words referring to the same concept or something entirely different? Other examples in English include words like soul, spirit, heart, mind, ghost, or flesh. Sometimes in the Old Testament, the Hebrew word *nephesh* is translated as "soul" and other times it's translated as "mind." Yet it's the same original word. Likewise, the word, *ruah* at times is translated as "spirit," at other times, as "soul," and sometimes it's even translated as "wind"!

What's a Trichotomist?

As skilled theologians examine these words and concepts, trying to systematize them in a way we can comprehend, they sometimes come to different conclusions. One school of theologians says all of these different words mean essentially the same thing, thus man is two parts, spirit and body. These are called dichotomists. Another school of theology recognizes a difference in the use and contexts of various words that seem to refer to three parts: body, soul, and spirit. These are considered trichotomists, and I hold to this theory based on a clear reading of 1 Thessalonians 5:23...

> 23 Now may the God of peace himself sanctify you completely, and may your whole spirit and soul and body be kept blameless at the coming of our Lord Jesus Christ.

Remember, the original language of the New Testament is Greek, so the meanings of these words are:

- *Pneuma* (spirit) – The part of you that relates to the eternal.
- *Psuche* (soul) – The seat of your mind, will, and emotions (also referred to as the "heart").
- *Soma* (body) – Your physical being.

This trichotomy of being is what sets you and me apart from all other creation. For instance, plants have a body, but no soul or spirit. Animals have a body and soul, but no spirit. Humans have a body, soul, and spirit. How do we know? When Adam and Eve were created, they were fully alive in body, soul, and spirit. In other words, they were perfectly healthy humans. They did not experience sickness or death, and they enjoyed perfect community with one another, naked and unashamed. They walked with God in beautiful harmony in the cool of the day. We read in Genesis 2:16–17…

> 16 … "You may surely eat of every tree of the garden, 17 but of the tree of the knowledge of good and evil you shall not eat, for in the day that you eat of it you shall surely die."

And what happened? Both the man and the woman took and ate, ushering in their own death. But in what ways did they die? The trichotomist would say that their spirits died instantly as they were cut off from God. Their souls (mind, will, and emotions) were corrupted as they understood good and evil, and their bodies were doomed to one day die on earth. And this is where you and I come into the picture. Apple seeds yield apple trees, lemon seeds produce lemon trees, and sinners reproduce sinners. So as a result, you and I were born physically alive, mentally corrupted, and spiritually dead.

Thanks be to God, that's not where the story ends. Jesus came to earth to redeem His children. We hear and understand the gospel, have a change of heart and mind (repentance), and we believe. Thus, we are "born again"! So what part of us is reborn?

Nicodemus raised this question in John 3:4 when he asked Jesus, *"How can a man be born when he is old? Can he enter a second time into his mother's womb and be born?"* Jesus responds in verse 6, *"That which is born of the flesh is flesh, and that which is born of the Spirit is spirit."* Upon faith in Jesus Christ, our spirits are made alive and born again. So today, if you are a follower of Jesus, this is your current state: Your body will one day die and be raised again. Until then, you'll struggle with the effect of sin. The number of your physical days are already determined and written in a book. You might say, *"Then why should I exercise and eat right?"* You can't affect the quantity of your life, but you can improve the quality.

And that is why Paul said: *Bodily discipline is of a little benefit.*

Your spirit, the part that came alive when you believed, is as saved as it will ever be. Your spiritual self is in the same position as the apostle Paul or the great Billy Graham. It is as eternally secure as Jesus Christ himself! His righteousness was imputed to your spirit. And that means that in ten million years, your spirit will not be any more saved than it is right now.

That is why Paul says in Ephesians 2:6, *We are already seated with Christ in the heavenlies…*

Lastly, your soul is a different matter altogether. Remember, your soul refers to your mind, will, and emotions.

These aspects of your being are fallen and affected by sin. They must be changed slowly over a lifetime.

This is what theologians refer to as "sanctification," and it's what Paul refers to in Romans 12:2 when he says,

> [2] Do not be conformed to this world, but be transformed by the *renewal of your mind,* that by testing you may discern what is the will of God, what is good and acceptable and perfect.

Your spirit is already made perfect, your body will be made perfect in the resurrection, and your mind is made perfect each day as you progressively subject your thoughts to God's thoughts. This is what Paul means in 2 Corinthians 10:5...

> [5] We destroy arguments and every lofty opinion raised against the knowledge of God, and take every thought captive to obey Christ.

The word picture is that of a Roman centurion holding a spear and taking a person prisoner until they submit to Caesar as Lord. We do the same with thoughts or ideas. We "take them captive" at spear point until they are submissive to the Lordship of Jesus Christ.

Responding to our Culture in Mind, Body, and Spirit

I never did well in school. I always struggled academically because I saw things differently than my teachers and professors. I didn't always agree with their take on American history or the elements of science. So, I would answer honestly (and I believe accurately), but they didn't accept my answers as truth. One day, I was making my case with a friend, explaining why I disagreed with a teacher's conclusion. My friend explained to me, *"That makes absolutely no difference. That is just simply not how the education system works. You are not graded on rightness or wrongness... you are graded on your ability to know and understand what the teacher is looking for, and to provide it."*

This was a revolutionary concept for me! In other words, it didn't matter if the teacher was wrong in my view. In that case, I am to provide the wrong answers when requested in order to receive a passing grade. In a similar way, this concept relates to our relationship with God, except of course the fact that He is never actually wrong. But in the way that sometimes, we are not sanctified to the degree that we comprehend His rightness. It's not uncommon for an unbeliever or a new believer to say, *"I don't see it that way."* That really has no bearing on the actual truth. Let God be true and every man a liar, Scripture says in Romans 3:4.

So if the battleground is in the mind and the weapons are ideas, take note of Paul's argument in 2 Corinthians 10:4–5 as a trichotomist...

> [4] For the weapons of our warfare are not of the flesh (*body*) but have divine power (*spirit*) to destroy strongholds (*in the soul—mind, will, emotions*). [5] We destroy arguments and every lofty opinion raised against the knowledge of God, and take every thought captive to obey Christ... [emphasis mine]

In light of the above passage, how do we respond when ideas like cultural Marxism or gender ideologies begin to affect us, our families, our churches, or our communities? They must be addressed with the body, soul, and spirit. First, let's consider the soul is made up of mind, will, and emotions. Do you see any observable changes that have made it possible for these ideas to take root in recent generations? How about the informational and technological revolution?

It's shocking to note that teens spend approximately nine hours a day absorbing media.[12] Ninety-one percent of teenagers go to bed with a device in their hands. And today, mobile devices account for 60 percent of online traffic[13] while computers and laptops are becoming increasingly obsolete.

I remember the first time I heard about a device called a modem that could dial into the Library of Congress and access thousands of books. Today, practically every book ever written can be accessed from a small device I carry around in my pocket. Not to mention every song ever recorded and every movie ever filmed!

Simultaneously, I can be connected wirelessly to anyone on the planet, regardless of their ideology, morality, or system of beliefs. And guess what? The vast majority of the gatekeepers to this cyberspace are cultural Marxists. It's crucial that we learn to filter the unmitigated absorption of ideas that come into our minds through modern technology.

So what's our defense? Unfortunately, it's impossible to create one. This space is moving and evolving and the enemy is taking advantage of it like never before. Satan makes Einstein look like a fool and he will outsmart you at every turn. We can't simply focus on defense in this battle, we must rather turn our attention toward offense.

Learn how to encourage others toward a robust spiritual walk. This is why a local church is so very important! Worship, teaching, community, and truth have a serious effect on our souls... and if you're not engaging in the church, you're losing the battle. But not only must we dive into a local church, we must master the Word of God.

Hebrews 4:12 says,

> For the word of God is living and active, sharper than any two-edged sword, piercing to the division of soul and of spirit...

Jesus battled Satan's ideas in the wilderness with God's Word from the book of Deuteronomy. Like Jesus, we must learn how to take ideas captive and ask, *"What does the Bible say?"*

Secondly, responding to our culture when it comes to the body is important as well. As Christians, we often assume that everything is spirit and soul. But we ought not to disregard the physical apparatus of the brain. Although ideas and thoughts form in the soul, the soul's primary tool is a physical organ. So a person may be receiving correct, biblical information, but they are not able to respond to it properly because of a physical or chemical issue.

Years ago, I heard about a man whose child was exhibiting emotions that didn't make sense. He would speak truth to his child, and although the child seemed to believe the truth, something was going on in the brain that seemed to short-circuit what his father was saying. After an intense season of prayer, my friend sensed the Lord say, *"Don't confuse symptoms with sins."* In other words, the behavior he was observing was a symptom of something rather than a sinful response to truth.

So, my friend and his wife began to talk to a Christian psychiatrist who helped tremendously. This doctor put the young person on a very low dose of medication called a norepinephrine reuptake inhibitor. Suddenly, the child was behaving appropriately and truth had a fighting chance.

Now, a word to the men. I get it. It's difficult to address issues of the soul or the mind. I've often found that a man will take all sorts of medications for physical issues, but when it comes to his brain, he says, *"I'll handle it myself."* But how do you know when you need help? If following normal spiritual disciplines and habits doesn't seem to be helping you like it helps others, it may be time to talk to someone. If people who know and love you are telling you that you need to talk to a professional, perhaps they are right. Depression, anxiety, addictions, and gender dysphoria are real mental issues with real effects. Don't turn to medicine first and/or medicine only, but stay aware of physical symptoms that can be treated successfully with means God has graciously made available.

Lastly, let's look at how to respond to these issues in the spirit. Your spirit is the most vital part of you, and thankfully, it is the most simple aspect of humanity to treat. You are either spiritually alive, or you're spiritually dead. It's truly as simple as that. Do you enjoy reading God's Word? Is it difficult for you to pray? These may be symptoms of a lack of spiritual life. The worse thing I could do for you is to help treat your soul, find a doctor to treat your body, yet leave you spiritually dead. And guess what else? It is pointless to treat your soul emotionally and your body physically while neglecting your spirit.

One of my favorite movies is titled *Analyze This,* starring Robert

De Niro and Billy Crystal. Robert De Niro plays a mafia boss who is experiencing severe anxiety and comes to a psychiatrist for help (Billy Crystal). Crystal's character says, *"What? Am I supposed to make you a happy, well-adjusted gangster?"* Today, I would say to you, what does it benefit a man if he finds mental health, physical strength, lives a long life, yet loses his soul for all eternity? My job is not to make you happy, well-adjusted spiritually dead human being. My job is to point you to the light of Jesus who can save your spirit and resurrect your very life.

Consider this: When Jesus died, He suffered mental anguish, physical anguish, and spiritual anguish... *for you.* He died fully and completely the death you were supposed to die. And three days later, He rose again. Take a moment to let that sink in. Seek to understand it and believe it. If this is news to you, allow your dead spirit to breathe and experience a new birth in Christ today. If this is a well-needed reminder, then rejoice today because you have life forever in Jesus, body, soul, and spirit.

Questions to consider:

1. How does understanding the original Greek language in 1 Thessalonians 5:23 shed light on how God created you? Is it difficult or easy for you to differentiate between your body, soul, and spirit?

2. In light of 2 Corinthians 10:5, what thoughts or ideas do you sometimes have to "take captive" in order to determine if they are God's ultimate truth? In what tangible ways can we filter ideas that enter our minds through modern technology?

3. Do you feel there is a negative stigma in your community toward chemical medications when it comes to mental health? Why do you think it's important to maintain physical health if our bodies aren't made to last anyway?

4. How does understanding the gospel give you ultimate hope and peace when it comes to the eternal perspective of your spirit?

CHAPTER SIX

LGBTQ++: THE PATH FORWARD

Reaching This Community with Both Truth and Compassion

There seems to be a common goal when it comes to various groups forming in today's society: A cultural revolution. And primary among these special interest groups is the coalition known as LGBTQ++ (Lesbian, Gay, Bisexual, Transgender, and Queer). The final two plus signs indicate that this community is growing indefinitely to include any number of alternatives that may emerge in the coming days.

According to Dr. Albert Mohler, the transgender revolution has reached a critical stage in which it now touches virtually every dimension of society.[14] Creators of entertainment seem eager to include transgender characters and actors in their productions. School systems in the U.S. now feature "gender identity" as a part of the curriculum, premised on the claim that even young children can decide their trans identity. And recently in Scotland, little boys and girls as young as four years old are now able to declare themselves as a different gender.[15] They can now legally change their names and their personal pronouns without parental consent or knowledge.

On top of this, virtually every collegiate and pro-sporting league is wrestling with questions surrounding how to approach trans athletes (biological males who have undergone hormone therapy, now claiming to be women).

Lia Thomas, born as Will Thomas, has now become a household name in the trans gender athlete debate. Early in his collegiate career, Will ranked 554 in the men's freestyle before his full transition into "Lia." Post "transition, » he's dominated the women's division in every category, and it hasn't even been close. And if you think this mentality only applies to certain pockets of society, you might be interested to know that The American Medical Association has recommended that hospitals no longer contain a box for "gender" on a person's birth certificate.

In addition, schools are going to great lengths to avoid gender stereotyping of kids. I recently heard of a school staff that began noticing boys playing with trucks at recess while girls were playing with dolls. One day, they made the decision to put all the little girls into one room with nothing but toy trucks. Fifteen minutes later while checking on the kids, one little girl whispered, *"Shhh! The little trucks are sleeping!"*

And lest we think that this is simply a west coast issue, take a visit to the University of Florida Health Center for Transgender Health in Jacksonville, FL. If a young person from four to eighteen years old wishes to change genders, there is a pediatric endocrinologist who will administer drugs in order to stop the natural process of maturity. The goal is to suppress the onset of puberty, remove hair, and even perform gender reassignment surgery on these young children. It seems to me that the American ideal has come down to this: *We have to become what we feel.*

Legendary UCLA basketball coach John Wooden said it this way: *"Being true to ourselves doesn't make us people of integrity. Charles Manson was true to himself and as a result he is rightly spending the rest of his life in prison. Ultimately, being true to our Creator gives us the purest form of integrity."*

Dr. Paul McHugh is the former psychiatrist-in-chief for Johns Hopkins Hospital and is the current distinguished service professor of psychiatry. He has written seven books and over one hundred peer-reviewed articles. Dr. McHugh maintains that despite the pressure of uninformed public opinion, psychologically transgenderism remains "a mental disorder that deserves understanding, treatment, and prevention."

He continues:

> "*This intensely felt sense of being transgendered constitutes a mental disorder in two respects. The first is that the idea of sex misalignment is simply mistaken—it does not correspond with physical reality. The second is that it can lead to grim psychological outcomes.*

> "*At the heart of the problem is confusion over the nature of the transgendered. 'Sex change' is biologically impossible. People who undergo sex-reassignment surgery do not change from men to women or vice versa. Rather, they become feminized men or masculinized women. Claiming that this is a civil-rights matter and encouraging surgical intervention is, in reality, to collaborate with and promote a mental disorder.*"[16]

Studies also show that children who believe themselves to be transgender change their minds and return to traditional roles *80 percent* of the time as their feelings dissipate. Sadly, those who remain irrevocably locked in their transgender identity through the process of gender reassignment surgery are *twenty* times more likely to commit suicide.[17]

And this is not an issue that only affects Hollywood stars or people standing on the corner of Times Square in New York City. No, it's a reality that is in some way touching every family in America, whether directly or indirectly. You may have friends with kids who are struggling with same-sex attraction, or young people in your church who have embraced this lifestyle completely. This next generation is confused, lost, and trying to find their way. Who's going to light the path?

Before we jump into our biblical text, let's define a few terms relevant to this chapter:

-    <u>Sex</u> – One's biological sex as assigned on a birth certificate. This signifies the arrangement of chromosomes and reproductive organs.

- <u>Gender</u> – The culture specific and non-scientific aspects of sex. For example, a baby announcement for a boy is going to be blue.

- <u>Gender Identity</u> – A person's sense of one's own gender.

- <u>Gender Dysphoria</u> – A psychological condition where a person has a perceived misalignment between their gender identity and their biological sex. (This is considered a psychological malady.)

- <u>Transgenderism</u> – When a person's gender identity does not align with their biological sex, and they seek to remedy that misalignment by external means.

How are Christians to respond to such a confused culture? And what does Scripture say that can guide us? Let's dive into a passage of Scripture that I believe gives us a paradigm for understanding what is happening, as well as a process for how to address the issue with those we love.

We'll start in Matthew 19:1–12 …

> [1] Now when Jesus had finished these sayings, he went away from Galilee and entered the region of Judea beyond the Jordan. [2] And large crowds followed him, and he healed them there. [3] And Pharisees came up to him and tested him by asking, "Is it lawful to divorce one's wife for any cause?"

The subject Jesus is addressing here was a common controversy among religious leaders in first-century Israel. It was the morality of divorce. According to the New American Commentary, the question asked reflects the intra-pharisaic debate between the schools of Shammai and Hillel concerning the correct interpretation of Deuteronomy 24:1.

In that passage, God apparently permitted divorce for *"anything indecent."* Yet, what constituted indecency was not defined. Shammai, placing the emphasis on "indecent," took this to refer to sexual unfaithfulness; Hillel, placing the emphasis on "anything," allowed divorce for as trivial an offense as a wife burning her husband's food.[18]

The Pharisees knew that if they could draw Jesus into their conflict, it would divide His followers and likely prove that He was a simple sectarian pundit rather than a prophet or, better yet, God's Messiah. But Jesus never fell into such traps. And I believe His careful response to this question speaks to the complex issues we face regarding the LGBTQ++ community.

A Doctrinal Foundation

First in this passage, Jesus provides a doctrinal foundation. He responds to questions about divorce by taking His listeners back to the beginning of creation. This is an important first step because there are clear principles in biblical interpretation. For instance, The Law of First Use says that God doesn't grant revelation frivolously, the first things He gave us were first for a reason. They set the norm for what follows.

> [4] He answered, "Have you not read that he who created them from the beginning made them male and female..."

Why is that significant? Because Jesus is pointing out the Creator's intention. Marriage and gender were not necessary evils, but rather the specific design of creation. And notice, implications are drawn from this design...

> [5] "... and said, 'Therefore a man shall leave his father and his mother and hold fast to his wife, and the two shall become one flesh'"? [6] So they are no longer two but one flesh. What therefore God has joined together, let not man separate.

It couldn't be clearer. The intention of the Creator was marriage between one man and one woman... for life.

> [7] They said to him, "Why then did Moses command one to give a certificate of divorce and to send her away?" [8] He said to them, "Because of your hardness of heart Moses allowed you to divorce your wives, but from the beginning it was not so..."

The provision of divorce was an *accommodation* due to our sinful, hard hearts, but it was not God's original intent. Then, Jesus, as God in the flesh, makes a comment that Moses never dared to make...

> [9] "And I say to you: whoever divorces his wife, except for sexual immorality, and marries another, commits adultery."

This is a new authoritative revelation directly from Jesus. If the divorce is due to biblical reasons, the innocent person may remarry. But if they call for a divorce frivolously and remarry, they are guilty of adultery.

A Cultural Illustration

After providing this doctrinal foundation, Jesus provides a cultural illustration.

> [10] The disciples said to him, "If such is the case of a man with his wife, it is better not to marry." [11] But he said to them, "Not everyone can receive this saying, but only those to whom it is given. [12] For there are eunuchs who

have been so from birth, and there are eunuchs who have been made eunuchs by men, and there are eunuchs who have made themselves eunuchs for the sake of the kingdom of heaven.

In this historical context, only one category existed of a male who was single and celibate for a lifetime—a eunuch. Eunuchs were typically slaves owned by royalty and often, they were taken from among the conquered peoples and forced into the king's service. In this day, kings had many wives and concubines, which comprised their Haram. The eunuch's job was to serve and protect the Haram. They were castrated to ensure that they could not pollute the royal bloodline. Typically, boys were made eunuchs in their preteen or early teenage years. This process of emasculation had devastating effects on young men's physical and emotional development. Their voice would fail to change at the onset of puberty and their physical development would be abnormal. Arms would grow far longer than was typical and the ears and nose would become enlarged. As a result, eunuchs were easy to identify.

The eunuch was the closest thing to a non-binary "gender identity" that people experienced in first-century Israel. Thus, the reason we are using this text to inform our current circumstances.

Eunuchs did not marry, procreate, or experience physical intimacy. So when the disciples mention, *"If such is the case of a man with his wife, it is better not to marry,"* the only category where this existed was among the eunuchs. Now, as Jesus addresses this divergent identity, He gives us categories that are helpful in our approach to the LGBTQ++ landscape in which we find ourselves.

With that said, being a eunuch was not, in and of itself, sinful. At times, it was even commendable. So, with that caveat of understanding, I believe we can use Jesus' teaching here to draw out a few principles.

Predisposed, Groomed, or Intentional?

The Predisposed – *"For there are eunuchs who have been so from birth..."*

Jesus points out that there are some people who, from birth, have had a different experience than the majority of people. They have been eunuchs since birth.

The original intention had already been established—God created male and female, and those two genders were to marry and procreate. Jesus also recognizes that the fall into sin has had some deep, lasting effects on all of creation. Some were eunuchs from birth, having been born without the natural desire for the opposite sex or the ability to procreate.

Here is a question to consider, *"Is it possible that due to the fall and the curse of sin, some people, from birth, are predisposed to struggle with particular temptations like same-sex attraction?"*

I would answer this question by saying yes, it seems that way. So the question is frequently raised, "If someone is predisposed to struggle with same-sex attraction, doesn't that make it okay?" The short answer is no. Everyone has predisposed weaknesses, particularly related to sexual temptations. Those who struggle with heterosexual temptation should not say, "God made me this way. Therefore, it is ok for me to sin." Instead, as Paul instructed in 1 Corinthians 9:27, we must discipline our bodies and keep them under control. Failure to do so makes one an adulterer, which Paul warns in 1 Corinthians 6, stands as evidence that we have not experienced conversion.

You can probably think of someone you know who has struggled most of their life with things that are unnatural. Does that mean you categorize that person and assign them over to a sin pattern for life? Of course not. It simply means that they will need discipleship, accountability, and direction in order to develop a normal sexual experience or to maintain purity in celibacy as a

Christ follower.

The Groomed *– "…and there are eunuchs who have been made eunuchs by men…"*

Here, Christ references a second category of eunuchs—those affected by something outside themselves, an event that has led to a divergent experience of gender and sexuality. In fact, this was the typical experience of the eunuch. The typical eunuch was identified for extraordinary abilities as a leader and manager. He was then castrated, making him a eunuch for the remainder of his life. This is what happened to Daniel the Prophet in the Old Testament.

In the same way, it is not uncommon for a person who identifies as LGBTQ++ to have experienced a traumatic encounter early in life, such as sexual abuse or early exposure to sexual material. Trauma like this can have a massive impact on one's normal phases of mental and emotional development.

Here are some specific things that work together in order to "groom" a person toward a certain identity:

- According to one study, 26.6 percent of girls and 5.1 percent of boys under the age of 18 experience sexual abuse or assault at the hands of an adult.[19]
- Many kids today are exposed to pornography younger than ever before.
- Florida Citizens Alliance has identified forty-four books found in public schools that indoctrinate kids according to the transgender agenda.
- Everywhere you look, people are stumbling over themselves trying to find the perfect non-binary personal pronouns so that they seem a little more progressive than the next company.

The Intentional *– "… and there are eunuchs who have made* *themselves eunuchs..."*

As I mentioned earlier, this is one of those occasions where a person made himself a eunuch for the Glory of God, and it was a commendable thing. This is comparable to the gift of celibacy that Paul describes in 1 Corinthians 7.

However, this third path to becoming a eunuch, I believe, may also inform our understanding of how some people enter into an LGBTQ++ lifestyle. The intentional path is what is referred to in Romans 1.

Romans 1:18–25 says,

> [18] For the wrath of God is revealed from heaven against all ungodliness and unrighteousness of men, who by their unrighteousness suppress the truth...

> [21] For although they knew God, they did not honor him as God or give thanks to him, but they became futile in their thinking, and their foolish hearts were darkened. [22] Claiming to be wise, they became fools, [23] and exchanged the glory of the immortal God for images resembling mortal man and birds and animals and creeping things. [24] *Therefore God gave them up in the lusts of their hearts to impurity, to the dishonoring of their bodies among themselves...*

Paul is speaking categorically about large segments of the human race. This passage could describe the decades that followed the Tower of Babel. Humanity spreads over the face of the earth, carrying with them the knowledge of God, the oral traditions handed down since the time of Noah. Each tribe knew of creation, they knew of the fall, they knew of God's judgment on the earth. They knew of the *proto-evangel* that first promised that one day the seed of the woman would crush the serpent's head, making all things right. Yet, one by one, they turned from the knowledge of God toward idolatry, and perverse sexuality soon followed.

What Paul describes in the macro sense, untold millions of people have experienced in the micro sense. Choosing to play with sins that play for keeps. Finding themselves caught up in something bigger than themselves. So grossly wrapped up in sin, that only the power of God can set them free.

Over the years, I have counseled countless individuals who pushed the limits of sexuality as teenagers; they dabbled in porn again and again until one day they discovered, in the words of B.B. King, "the thrill is gone." The old high wasn't there anymore; it would take something more salacious, more perverse, to give them the same rush they had previously experienced.

When this occurs, a person's nature becomes warped. They crave things that should sicken them. Like a dog returns to his vomit, they go back again and again.

The good news is, there is hope. Jesus can heal and free a person from the enemy's strongest chains. It takes time. You don't get into this situation overnight, and freedom is not always instantaneous. But there is freedom to be experienced.

What's the Path Forward?

"Let the one who is able to receive this receive it..." (Matthew 19:12)

No doubt, there are some strange things that have happened as a result of the fall. But God's intention and design are the goals we should be moving toward. We're told that not everyone is able to receive this, but for those that can, here are three things to remember when approaching friends with these struggles.

First and foremost, love them. Never forget that a person is far more than their sexual identity. Approach this person with the understanding that the number one problem is not the fact that they are gay or trans. It's that they're separated from Jesus. This is the same problem every human on earth faces, apart from God's grace. Now, what do we know about the love of God? It's patient. It understands that these things are deeply rooted and are not easy to walk away from.

Next, listen. People who find themselves in the LGBTQ++ community have gotten there somehow. And more often than not, they are hurting. You've probably heard the saying, *"Nobody cares how much you know, until they know how much you care."* This rings true. Thirdly, lead. Speak the truth in love and gently guide them toward freedom in Christ. It is not loving to accommodate an illusion; it *is* loving to offer truth in a gentle way.

In closing, don't forget that this battle begins in the home. You simply can't afford to be an absentee parent from an emotional standpoint in the lives of your kids. It is vitally important that you have open, honest, regular conversations about these issues. Be sure of this: If you don't talk to them about it, someone else will. And they very well may not have your child's best interest at heart.

Questions to consider:

1. Have you seen a rapid decline in healthy and biblical standards of sexuality/gender identity in the last decade? In what ways?

2. How has the LGTBQ++ mindset and agenda impacted you or someone you know? How can we better understand this community in order to reach them with the grace and truth of Christ?

3. Many times, Christians are seen as being harsh or judgmental on this issue. How can we tangibly love others while maintaining the truth and conviction of God's Word? When or where have you seen this done effectively?

CHAPTER SIX

CROSS-CULTURAL EVANGELISM

Understanding Other Worldviews for the Sake of the Gospel

If our vision is to reach our culture—and the next generation —with the truth of God's Word, sharing the gospel is a non-negotiable. It's God's Plan A! But the truth is, engaging in intelligent conversations with people of other religions can sometimes seem daunting. Just ask your kids. They're growing up in a world more culturally diverse than ever before. So even though it may feel daunting, remember that we're in it together and God has called us to this historical moment. The most important thing to remember is that thankfully, He doesn't leave us alone to figure this out. We have the Holy Spirit of the Living God in us to guide us into all truth and give us the words to say. And as we study other religions and prepare a proper defense for our faith, we can learn a whole lot from the apostle Paul in the book of Acts.

Let's dive into Acts 17:14–15:

> [14] Then the brothers immediately sent Paul off on his way to the sea, but Silas and Timothy [15] Those who conducted Paul brought him as far as Athens, and after receiving a command for Silas and Timothy to come to him as soon as possible, they departed.

As you can see from this passage, Paul is alone in Athens. How much trouble could he possibly cause?

Athens was already a very old city in Paul's day, over 4,000 years old. Named for the goddess Athena, the city had been the home of Socrates, Plato, Aristotle, and Alexander the Great, just to name a few notable figures. At one time, Athens had boasted a few hundred thousand residents, but by Paul's day, that number had dwindled to less than 50,000. Regardless, Athens still held a prominent place in the Roman imagination. Religiously, the Athenians were polytheistic (believing in many gods). Culturally, they were pluralistic (believing that many beliefs could and should be held at once, even if they were contradictory). Athens was a supposedly "open-minded" university town with a rich history. In practice, all the polytheistic worship and pluralistic worldviews led to one of the most perverse cultures imaginable.

In Acts 17:16, we read,

> [16] Now while Paul was waiting for them at Athens, his spirit was provoked within him as he saw that the city was full of idols.

Here, the Greek word Luke uses to describe Paul's inner turmoil is *parōxyneto.* It conveys the idea of being "stirred or sharpened to a point of exasperation." One theologian described Paul's reaction as a spiritual seizure! The apostle simply couldn't believe the spiritual state of Athenian culture—and he couldn't sit by without offering them the truth and hope of the gospel. So he responds in verse 17:

> [17] So he reasoned in the synagogue with the Jews and the devout persons, and in the marketplace every day with those who happened to be there.

This verse describes three categories of people Paul sought to reach with the gospel. First, the Jews, those who were raised on the Law of Moses and the Psalms of David. Next, devout persons, this includes people like Lydia. They knew of the God of the Jews, but they had stopped short of full commitment and conversion to Judaism. Lastly, Paul reached out to those in the marketplace. This group exemplifies the vague spirituality of the first century. It was not entirely unspiritual or irreligious. As a matter of fact, there were many customized religions in Athens.

The Roman historian and natural philosopher Pliny wrote that more than 3,000 statues dotted the landscape of the city.[20] And the Roman author Petronius quipped that it was easier to find a god than a man in Athens.[21]

Then verse 18 reads,

> [18] Some of the Epicurean and Stoic philosophers also conversed with him.

The epicureans believed that life should be lived for a person's maximum pleasure. Yes, they believed in a plurality of gods, but they argued that these gods remained distant and unconcerned with human affairs. So life, in their estimation, was best treated as a pleasure cruise. They did have one fly in their ointment, however. Death. How can you thoroughly enjoy life knowing death is imminent? And who knows what follows death?

The other group of philosophers Paul interacted with were stoics. Stoicism was founded in ancient Greece on the teaching of Zeno. In contrast to Epicurean philosophy, stoicism taught that you could achieve the ideal life by freeing yourself of extreme passion and emotions. For example, if you found out today that you won five million dollars, as a stoic, you would respond with a measured, balanced acknowledgment of the facts. It would not inflame your passions one way or another. Or worse, if your child was murdered on the way home, you would simply accept it as the will of the gods. Two extreme ideas, neither one reflected the truth of the gospel. So what did these epicurean and stoic philosophers make of Paul's Christianity?

Acts 17:18b says:

> [18] ... Others said, "He seems to be a preacher of foreign divinities"—because he was preaching Jesus and the resurrection.

This was the charge leveled against Socrates years earlier for which he was executed. So it was no small accusation! No wonder the citizens took Paul to the Areopagus—a stone outcropping just under the acropolis overlooked by the Parthenon. Greek Mythology taught that this was the place in which Aries was put on trial for the murder of Poseidon's son. It was the legal center of Athens. The ruling council here acted as the university board, legal jury, and police force. Paul stood on dangerous ground.

Acts 17:19–21 reads:

> [19] And they took him and brought him to the Areopagus, saying, "May we know what this new teaching is that you are presenting? [20] For you bring some strange things to our ears. We wish to know therefore what these things mean." [21] Now all the Athenians and the foreigners who lived there would spend their time in nothing except telling or hearing something new.

Competent Conversations

Paul's sermon that follows, details three key principles for bringing the gospel to those with a different worldview. First, we must have competent conversations. Paul provides a beautiful picture of this strategy by using three illustrations from Greek writers in his opening statement beginning in Acts 17: 22...

> [22] So Paul, standing in the midst of the Areopagus, said: "Men of Athens, I perceive that in every way you are very religious."

When Paul says "very religious" he employs an extremely rare Greek word famously used by the Greek dramatist Aeschylus in his play, *The Eumenides*, which means "The Furies." It's like Paul borrowed a buzz word that the Greeks would have recognized. And it's well within reason to imagine that Paul had actually read *The Eumenides* in his efforts to understand Greco-Roman culture and reach them with the gospel.

You see this strategy continued if you jump ahead to verses 27–28:

> [27] ... that they should seek God, and perhaps feel their way toward him and find him. Yet he is actually not far from each one of us, [28] for
>
> "'In him we live and move and have our being';
>
> as even some of your own poets have said,
>
> "'For we are indeed his offspring.'"

Here, Paul begins quoting thinkers and artists from Greco-Roman culture. The first quote comes from a poem written by a Cretan called Epimenedes. In the poem, the author denounces his fellow Cretans for their claim that Zeus was actually buried in Crete. His point is that if what the people believed about Zeus' divinity were true, then the thought that he was dead and buried in Crete was utterly ridiculous.

You can already begin to see the segue Paul is building to speak of the gospel and the resurrected Christ.

Then, in verse 28, Paul quotes a poem written by the stoic philosopher Aratus. Strategic, right? Paul knows that his audience has no biblical foundation whatsoever. These people had no category for the authority and sufficiency of Scripture. So Paul meets them where they're at—quoting the cultural influences that shaped Athenian thought. In the same way, if we are seeking to reach across a culture to connect others to the gospel, we have to take the time to acquaint ourselves with their worldview. It's been said that Billy Graham's evangelical team would spend months prior to a crusade studying the culture of that city.

The key is to know the culture and understand its people without being overly enamored by it. You and I are called to be in the world, yes, but not of it.

In contrast to Paul's approach, Christians today tend to respond to culture with one of two extremes: We either withdraw or we accommodate. The tendency to withdraw is illustrated by the family who steers clear of schools, media, technology, and anything else that smacks of the wider culture. In essence, these believers remain in a self-made bubble, content to simply wait inside their homes for the rapture to come. Accommodation on the other hand occurs when the Christian waves the white flag and says, *"If you can't beat 'em, join 'em!"* These believers lose their prophetic voice as they blur the differences between a biblical and a secular worldview. Having softened the rough edges of biblical truth, they lose their right to speak into the culture and call people to life-saving repentance.

Cultural Contradictions

Instead of withdrawing or accommodating, Paul engages for the sake of Christ. Today, God is calling you and me to do the same. Not only must we prepare for competent conversations, but we must recognize the cultural contradictions.

Jump back a few verses to Acts 17:23...

> [23] "For as I passed along and observed the objects of your worship, I found also an altar with this inscription, 'To the unknown god.' What therefore you worship as unknown, this I proclaim to you."

Paul had a thoroughly developed biblical worldview, and this enabled him to clearly spot the inconsistencies in other systems of belief. According to the Athenian worldview, there was a god for everything. In fact, there were over 300,000 gods in all! Even with so many deities, the Athenians worried they may have overlooked a god, so just in case, they erected an altar to an "unknown" god. Paul saw this as an open door to a gospel conversation, and he took it.

Keep reading in verses 24–26:

> [24] "The God who made the world and everything in it, being Lord of heaven and earth, does not live in temples made by man, [25] nor is he served by human hands, as though he needed anything, since he himself gives to all mankind life and breath and. [26] And he made from one man every nation of mankind to live on all the face of the earth..."

Remember, the Athenians worldview rested on polytheistic religion. The universe encompassed many gods, and they believed that different gods were responsible for creating different people groups. But Paul says, *"No! God started with one man, and all came from him."*

Paul continues his argument in the next verse, utilizing the Greek affinity for logic. He appeals to their reason, arguing that when it comes to the origins of man, the more complex being would necessarily produce the less complex being.

> [29] "Being then God's offspring, we ought not to think that the divine being is like gold or silver or stone, an image formed by the art and imagination of man."

The God who created all of humanity cannot be less complex than human beings. Simply put, He's not a block of wood!

As you engage people with different worldviews, remember that each theory or religion must answer four questions:

1) Origin: Where did we come from?

2) Meaning: Why are we here?
3) Morality: What are we to do?
4) Destiny: What happens when we die?

If you are going to win your friends, coworkers, family members, and neighbors to Jesus, you must be able to competently and accurately understand how this person's worldview answers each of those questions.

Consider atheistic evolution as an example.

1) Origin: Where did we come from?

   All living things evolved from a single-celled organism (Darwin's "universal common ancestor") over a process billions of years in the making.

2) Meaning: Why are we here?

   There is no answer to "why"; we are simply here.

3) Morality: What are we to do?

   There is no basis for morality, because morality depends upon the revelation of absolute truth.

4) Destiny: What happens when we die?

   We simply cease being.

This worldview answers the question of origin, but notice that it has no answer for meaning. Further, how do you form a foundation for morality in this worldview? You can't, but do you know what's interesting? I have never met an evolutionist who does not hold to some form of morality to which they believe all people are accountable. Do you see the contradiction?

If there is no reason, no God, no destiny, then why do I feel warmly about my children? Why would I risk my life for theirs? More so, why would I risk my own life to save *your* children? Every person has some type of moral system and on occasion expresses moral outrage… why is that? Could it be that you are an image bearer of God, with His law written on your heart from the beginning of time?

Constant Comparison

In order to reach the culture, not only must you hold competent conversations and recognize cultural contradictions, you must hold the gospel in constant comparison. Look at Paul's approach in Acts 17:30…

> [30] "The times of ignorance God overlooked, but now he commands all people everywhere to repent…"

Consider that statement. Paul stands in the capital city of intelligence and education, the Oxford, Harvard, or Yale of his day and says, *"Your greatest problem is ignorance."* Wow! Here, Paul attacks the primary idol of Athens: knowledge. In essence, he says, *"You don't know what you don't know."*

Then in verse 31, he says:

> [31] "… because he has fixed a day on which he will judge the world in righteousness by a man whom he has appointed; and of this he has given assurance to all by raising him from the dead."

Paul centers every thought, assertion, and claim on one person— Jesus Christ. He tells them that one day, Jesus will judge their idols. Then he boldly says, *"Oh, by the way, Jesus will judge you, too."*

How do you think they reacted to Paul's words?

> [32] Now when they heard of the resurrection of the dead, some mocked. But others said, "We will hear you again about this." [33] So Paul went out from their midst. [34] But some men joined him and believed, among whom also were Dionysius the Areopagite and a woman named Damaris and others with them.

Paul sought to understand the culture. Recognize its contradictions. Then engage it with the gospel. As a result, three new categories of people developed. Those who mocked the gospel, those who wanted to hear more of it, and those who believed it.

Among those who believed were Dionysius and a woman named Damaris. Dionysius was apparently on the judging council that day in Athens. He was saved and history tells us that later he became the first pastor of the church at Athens. Interestingly, today the Acropolis is not the highest point in Athens, there is actually one point higher, a church. And would you believe this? Today, 98 percent of the city of Athens considers themselves Christian.

As you engage those around you with the truth of the gospel, above all else, remember that the Holy Spirit is with you and will give you the words to say. Do your homework, answer the four questions of origin, meaning, morality, and destiny, and simply share your story of how the truth of God's Word has changed your life.

Then leave the results to the one who is over it all.

Questions to consider:

1. Do you feel more equipped or intimidated when it comes to engaging those with other worldviews?

2. Has God placed anyone in your path recently whom you might engage in a competent conversation about the gospel?

3. How can you begin instilling the four questions of origin, meaning, morality, and destiny into your children or loved ones? Can you identify like Paul those who mock, those who want to hear more, and those who believe? Where do you stand?

CHAPTER EIGHT

LOVING PEOPLE WHEN IT'S HARD

Obeying the "Upside-down" Command of Jesus: Love Your Enemies!

Certain aspects of the Christian faith are typically accepted and even praised in a civilized society, regardless of your religion. One such principle is the biblical command to honor your father and mother. Think about it: No matter what religion you hold to or what "holy" book you esteem, you will find some form of teaching that relates to honoring your parents. In addition to honoring your parents, some form of the "Golden Rule" can be found in Judaism, Hinduism, and even Islam. Likewise, you'll also find commands to help the poor and needy in almost all religious creeds.

Yet there are certain teachings that do in fact set Christianity apart from all other religions. Some of these concepts include the exclusivity and divine nature of Christ, salvation coming to us by grace through faith alone, and the command of Jesus to love your enemies. I don't know about you, but that last one is especially hard—the people on my enemy list got there for good reason! The truth is, Jesus motions His nail-scarred hand toward the person you most dislike, distrust, and disapprove of and says, *"Go love that one."*

Let's back up a little. If you remember from the book of Genesis, Adam was given dominion over the entire earth. He subjugated that kingdom to Satan by trusting the word of the serpent over the word of God. God then promised that He would send a seed, a male descendant of Adam, who would crush Satan's head... in doing so, He would reclaim and restore all that Adam had lost.

The drama of the Old Testament continues to unfold as mankind awaits that coming seed, the King, the one and only Messiah. This great anticipation of the ages was met with a baby's cry in that tiny town of Bethlehem. Christ came as the King of all kings, and through His death and resurrection, He won back what Adam had lost. And in so doing, made redemption possible for the human race. Then He called His disciples together in Matthew 28:18–20 and said this:

> [18] And Jesus came and said to them, "All authority in heaven and on earth has been given to me. [19] Go therefore and make disciples of all nations, baptizing them in the name of the Father and of the Son and of the Holy Spirit, [20] teaching them to observe all that I have commanded you. And behold, I am with you always, to the end of the age."

So there you have it. Jesus has been given legal and divine authority over every single realm of existence. And each individual within those realms has one job: Obedience.

Now there are four realms of existence addressed in the Bible: The self, the family, the church, and the state. Although Jesus is Lord over all four, He relates to each realm differently. Because each of these realms has a vested responsibility. For instance, there are some things the state can do that the church can't, such as capital punishment. There are things the family can do, but the church can't, such as corporal punishment of children. And there are things the church can do that the state can't. For example, administering the means of grace.

The "self" exists within the context of all three realms.

In the Sermon on the Mount, Jesus is addressing the individual, the self. He is telling the crowd how He wants His followers to deal with personal offenses. Now, He's not speaking to the national defense or personal defense of your family or church.

He's giving us as believers a kingdom strategy for responding to personal offenses.

Loving your enemies is not some "holier-than-thou" command. It is a God-given mandate for advancing the agenda of His Kingdom on earth. And like all good strategies, if we implement it, it will work!

Is it okay to have enemies?

Take a look at Luke 6:27–36:

[27] "But I say to you who hear, Love your enemies..."

In order to love our enemies, we must have a category called "enemy." There must be people in the world whom you look at and say, *"Yep, that's my enemy."* Now, if you are a Christian in Western culture, that probably makes you uncomfortable. Christians today commonly perceive Jesus as the great unifier, not as someone to divide others into negative categories. The truth is that many Christians have accepted some anemic version of Jesus handed down by cowardly preachers afraid to preach the whole Bible.

Let me explain.

Over the last few decades, preaching in the American church has reflected something Christian Smith calls "Moralistic Therapeutic Deism."[22] In practice, this looks like a preacher cherry-picking verses that echo the self-help message of the secular book he or she prefers to read, presenting it to you as the whole counsel of God. This, combined with biblical illiteracy, means that we have no idea how we are to behave in the ordinary challenges of life. I fear we're raising a generation of Christians who've been taught to zero in on teachings of Jesus like *"Don't judge..."* while failing to interpret that verse in light of its context. Before Jesus tells

Christians not to judge, He tells us to identify certain people as our enemies and that requires judgement.

Scripture is filled with references to a category of people called enemies. For instance…

Philippians 3:18 (NASB1995) speaks of enemies of the gospel when Paul says:

> [18] For many walk, of whom I often told you, and now tell you even weeping, that they are enemies of the cross of Christ…

And he says of unbelieving Jews in Romans 11:28 (NASB1995):
> [28] From the standpoint of the gospel they are enemies for your sake…

Later, to the occultic, street magician Bar-Jesus, Paul says in Acts 13:10 (NASB1995):

> [10] "You who are full of all deceit and fraud, you son of the devil, you enemy of all righteousness…"

Christ Himself says in Matthew 10:36 (NASB1995) that in the last days,

> [36] a man's enemies will be the members of his household.

Consider the fact that our Lord was perfect in every way, the very essence of holiness. Yet He had a plethora of enemies, to such a degree that they ultimately put Him to death. If that is true of Jesus Christ, God in the flesh, how much more will they persecute those of us who are far from perfect, yet preaching His same message?

2 Timothy 3:12 tells us,

> [12] Indeed, all who desire to live a godly life in Christ Jesus will be persecuted…

Earthly enemies are assumed. Not because we declare them to be enemies, but because they set themselves up against the Kingdom of Christ. Yet these are the very people Christ calls you and me to love—so that through Him, our enemies might become our brothers and sisters.

Identifying Your True Enemy

Here's a newsflash: Your spouse or ex-spouse is not your actual enemy. Nor is your boss or that friend who is often slandering you in front of others.

These are misidentified enemies.

Remember that this battle is not against other people, but rather against Satan and his demons. Satan is in fact our ultimate foe, as

Ephesians 6:12 says:

> [12] For we do not wrestle against flesh and blood, but against the rulers, against the authorities, against the cosmic powers over this present darkness, against the spiritual forces of evil in the heavenly places.

Now ask yourself, why are we as Christians in this battle? What are we fighting for? You and I are fighting for the enslaved hearts and minds of people. This is why you must not misidentify your ultimate enemy. If you begin to view another person as your enemy, you are neglecting the possibility of that person repenting. Remember Saul of Tarsus? He positioned himself as an enemy of the Church but then met Jesus. This could certainly happen to a person who treats you like an enemy. How would you feel if it did? Perhaps we misidentify our ultimate "enemy" because that makes it easier not to pursue their salvation.

I once heard of a sermon a preacher delivered titled "Love your Enemies." After the message, the preacher asked, *"How many of you are willing to forgive all your enemies?"* About half held up their hands. He then repeated his question, and about 80 percent held up their hands. He then repeated his question a third time, and all responded, except one elderly lady named Mrs. Jones. The pastor then asked, *"Mrs. Jones, are you not willing to forgive your enemies?"* To which she replied, *"I don't have any."* *"Mrs. Jones, that is very unusual. How old are you?"* the pastor asked. *"Ninety-three,"* she replied. *"Mrs. Jones, please come down and tell the congregation how a person cannot have an enemy in the world?"* It was then that she tottered down the aisle and said, *"It's rather easy, I just outlived them all."*

The moral of the story is that unless you outlive every last one of your enemies, as long as you are following Jesus, you will have some adversaries! But never forget who your true enemy is.

Your God-given Strategy

Christians don't need to wonder how we should respond to our enemies. Christ has made that quite clear. Not only do you and I have enemies, but we have a clear mandate to love them. Isn't that a relief? You don't have to guess or worry. You don't even have to pray about it. King Jesus has given us our instructions.

Keep reading in Luke 6:27–29:

> [27b] "Do good to those who hate you, [28] bless those who curse you, pray for those who abuse you. [29] To one who strikes you on the cheek, offer the other also…"

In Jewish communities at this time, you would insult someone by backhanding them on the cheek. What Jesus is saying here is this: If someone insults you, let them. He is not saying to never defend yourself. And He is certainly not forbidding you to defend the helpless. He is saying, *"Don't return insult for insult."*

Take a look at the rest of the passage:

> [29] …and from one who takes away your cloak do not withhold your tunic either. [30] Give to everyone who begs

from you, and from one who takes away your goods do not demand them back. [31] And as you wish that others would do to you, do so to them.

Notice, Jesus isn't commanding you to "feel" any particular way toward your enemies. Love, in this case, as in most cases in the New Testament, is more of a verb than a noun. It carries with it the idea of what you *do* to or for someone.

So here are five things Jesus says to do to those who are hard to love:

- Do good to them. Be intentional and creative.
- Bless them. Take the initiative and speak well to them and about them.
- Pray for them. Go to God on their behalf and ask Him to soften your heart.
- Don't retaliate against them. Vengeance belongs to the Lord.
- Show them generosity. Christianity is not transactional. We don't give in order to get. We give, even to our enemies, because we have received.

Now if this is how we love our enemies, how are we to love our friends? At least this much, right?

> [32] "If you love those who love you, what benefit is that to you? For even sinners love those who love them. [33] And if you do good to those who do good to you, what benefit is that to you? For even sinners do the same. [34] And if you lend to those from whom you expect to receive, what credit is that to you? Even sinners lend to sinners, to get back the same amount. [35] But love your enemies, and do good, and lend, expecting nothing in return, and your reward will be great..."

That sounds like a guarantee from God to me. If you bless your enemies, God will bless you. It doesn't say when or how, but you can count on it. In fact, I would say some of God's greatest blessings are reserved for those who obey this principle. Why? Because it's the life force of the gospel. Forgiven people forgive people. Forgiveness experienced results in forgiveness expressed. Jesus says that if we obey Him in this way, He has our back.

Not to mention...

> [35b] ... and you will be sons of the Most High, for he is kind to the ungrateful and the evil. [36] Be merciful, even as your Father is merciful.

You wouldn't believe how many times I've heard these words in my hometown: *"I don't know which one you are, but you must be one of those Terrys."* Our family looks a certain way. We're all relatively tall men with similar facial features. In the same way, when you are kind to an enemy, people say, *"I don't know which one you are, but you must be one of those Christians."* Why? Because that's what Christians do. We act like our Father. He is good to everyone, even to the point of saving His own enemies and adopting them as children. What ridiculous grace! Oh, the riches of God's love.

I've experienced ministry around the world in the streets of Cuba, Tegu Honduras, Guatemala, Albania, and Israel. No matter where I go, one of the things I've found to be true is that God has a habit of winning over His enemies. In our culture today, if the future of the Church of Christ as a Kingdom Outpost is to be bright, it won't be because of our large buildings; it will be because we are people of grace among enemies who desperately need the same love that saved us.

Questions to consider:

1. According to the description in this chapter, is there someone in your life whom you might label as an enemy? What did this person do to receive that title? Are you harboring resentment toward this person? Take a moment to ask God to speak to your heart on this matter.

2. How might thinking of your "battle" in terms of spiritual forces rather than specific people help you love others more fully?

3. How can your choice to love your enemies be seen as an offering to the Lord? Does this change your perspective?

CHAPTER NINE

HELPING YOUR CHILDREN NAVIGATE BABYLON

Principles from the Life of Daniel... And How They Apply to Our Culture Today

Looking at the state of the world today—and the state of culture in America—it's easy to feel like things have never been this bad. Many Christian parents especially worry that their children are growing up in one of the most hostile and immoral cultures any generation has faced. And while these are certainly difficult days, the truth is that God's people have had to stand on the truth against the tide of secular culture for millennia.

And that fact should encourage us because other believers have stood where we stand... and they triumphed.

The book of Daniel provides Christians with a powerful and practical manual for keeping their faith in a hostile culture. But in order to understand it, let's first talk about how we study the Bible.

The word Bible comes from the Latin word *Biblia* which means, "A collection of Holy Books." So, the Bible is a book of books that tells one unfolding story of who God is along with His plan to redeem those who would believe. Each time you study a new book of the Bible, it is important to determine the genre of the particular book you're reading. Because while your Bible is ultimately one story by one author, God used forty different human authors writing in a wide variety of literary genres over a period of 1,600 years.

When reading the Bible, it's important to allow for a mental shift when moving in and out of different genres represented. We're accustomed to doing this in modern writings. For example, when you read the newspaper, you make a mental shift when you move from an editorial into the comics, and then again as you read the sports section. Each is uniquely written and each assumes the reader knows something about its genre. But when people read the Bible, they often fail to realize it is a similar compilation. That's why many of us lose interest and fall off the wagon once we reach the book of Leviticus!

Genesis and Exodus are both historical narratives while Leviticus is more of a legal discourse. It's a book that has to be read and understood in a different way than if you were simply reading a story about history. Then there's the book of Daniel. This book contains two different genres. Chapters 1 through 6 are historical narratives (the fiery furnace, the lion's den, etc.) and chapters 7 through 12 are apocalyptic discourse, one of the most difficult types of literature to read. In many ways, understanding Daniel is the key to understanding the book of Revelation.

The prophecies of Daniel are so specific that nonbelievers argue against the possibility of a human writing about future events in such detail. Liberal scholars claim that the book of Daniel must have been written as if it were prophecy, after the fact. But as those who have traveled to Israel might observe, the fragments and quotes of the Dead Sea scrolls give evidence that Daniel was written well before the events recorded ever took place.

Daniel is the long-distance runner of the Old Testament. This book begins in his youth, in 605 B.C. when Daniel was taken captive in Babylon, and concludes in his senior adult years. His story begins as a victim of human trafficking and ends with him leading the most powerful man in the world to faith in the God of Israel. One day, you'll meet a man in heaven named Nebuchadnezzar… and he will be there because of Daniel.

Daniel in Babylon

God in His judgement removed Israel from their land, but God in His mercy left men like Daniel among them so that the light of revelation would shine, even in a foreign land.

Daniel 1:1–21 tells us,

> ¹ In the third year of the reign of Jehoiakim king of Judah, Nebuchadnezzar king of Babylon came to Jerusalem and besieged it.

Nebuchadnezzar, king of Babylon was one of the greatest monarchs of ancient times. He was the predominant leader of what is called the Neo-Babylonian Empire—the capital of modern-day Iraq. Nebuchadnezzar led a great expansion of Babylon's territory along with extensive building campaigns, including the hanging gardens of Babylon, one of the seven wonders of the ancient world.

Nebuchadnezzar had just conquered Egypt at the battle of Carchemish in June of 605 B.C. when, while on his way home, he decided to go ahead and besiege Jerusalem as well.

> ² And the Lord gave Jehoiakim king of Judah into his hand, with some of the vessels of the house of God. And he brought them to the land of Shinar, to the house of his god, and placed the vessels in the treasury of his god.

Note that Scripture says, "The Lord gave" Jehoiakim, king of Judah into the hand of Nebuchadnezzar. This wasn't simply geo-politics or military expansion; this was the divine judgement of God.

He lifted his protective hand of mercy and used Babylon to employ his punitive hand of judgement.

> ³ Then the king commanded Ashpenaz, his chief

> eunuch, to bring some of the people of Israel, both of
> the royal family and of the nobility, [4] youths without
> blemish, of good appearance and skillful in all wisdom,
> endowed with knowledge, understanding learning, and
> competent to stand in the king's palace, and to teach
> them the literature and language of the Chaldeans.

It was customary in Babylonian foreign policy that when they conquered a people, they took the best of the best from that population to make them palace servants. The fact that Daniel was included in this group suggests that he may have been in the kingly line, or at the very least among the nobility of Israel.

So, these exceptional young people were going to be given an exceptional education and training. Take a look at verse 5:

> [5] The king assigned them a daily portion of the food that
> the king ate, and of the wine that he drank. They were to
> be educated for three years, and at the end of that time
> they were to stand before the king. [6] Among these were
> Daniel, Hananiah, Mishael, and Azariah of the tribe of
> Judah.

Here they are, enrolled in Babylon University and beginning the process of indoctrination in the ways of this culture. They were well on their way to a Babylonian worldview as they would be taught to worship the demonic Babylonian idols and hold to a wicked, perverted Babylonian standard of morality.

Sound familiar? Can you relate to that scenario as a parent today?

In the New Testament, we are taught that the spirit of Babylon still exists and will have influence over much of the world in the last days. In Revelation 17:5, this demonic spirit is described as *"Babylon the great, mother of prostitutes and of earth's abominations."* This is the spirit of rebellion against a holy God. It's the central rebellion of man in his efforts to usurp the King of the universe and place himself on the throne. Make no mistake, this spirit has found a foothold in every kingdom on earth, whether it's Sodom & Gomorrah, Nazi Germany, North Korea, Iran, or America. It manifests itself in things like cartels, human trafficking, political platforms, media, entertainment, social media, and education. Daniel faced it. Christians since have faced it. And you and I face it today. So how do we stand strong? And how do we help our kids do the same?

Three Keys to Standing Strong in Babylon

The first thing we want to do when living in a Babylonian culture is to develop authentic, intentional Christian friendships. This is the type of relationship Daniel and his friends enjoyed while living in the demonically influenced environment of Babylon.

Babylon held to many laws that would make it nearly impossible for these men to stand for the one true God, but they failed to take into account the fact that they were not separated from each other. After all, you can stand a lot when you're standing together! Having a "tribe" and inner circle like Daniel's is vital when your beliefs and convictions land you in a minority. How does this translate into practice? Join a life-giving, Bible-preaching church. Immerse yourself in the life of the church and build your schedule around it. Regardless of where you find community in school, work, sports, clubs, etc., find a church community that preaches the Bible, stands for truth, and proclaims Jesus as the only way to heaven. Don't' get caught up in the style of worship or the facility. Pay more attention to whether or not the preacher is preaching God's Word. I am firmly convinced that there would be no Daniel if there had been no Hananiah, Mishael, and Azariah. You and I need godly, gospel-centered community in order to thrive as lights in a dark world.

Tim Keller says of this passage, *"Don't assimilate, don't separate, but be deeply involved and engaged in the life of the city (Babylon)."* Love the city of man for the sake of the city of God. But here's the thing: Too many Christians find their gospel community and retreat from the culture, huddling up together just waiting for the rapture. But that's not what God calls us to. Instead, you and I are called to turn our little crews into one big army and take back the city for the glory of Christ.

The second thing you need to do while living in Babylon is protect your Christian identity. Read verse 6 again:

> ⁶ Among these were Daniel, Hananiah, Mishael, and Azariah of the tribe of Judah.

These are all good, godly, Hebrew names that speak of their relation to Yahweh, the one true God.

But since the rulers of Babylon were in charge, they instead gave them names associated with Babylonian demonic idols. And changing your name in this sense changes your core identity...

> ⁷ And the chief of the eunuchs gave them names: Daniel he called Belteshazzar, Hananiah he called Shadrach, Mishael he called Meshach, and Azariah he called Abednego.

Let's look at how these names speak to the core identity of these men:

Hebrew Name	Babylonian Name
Daniel: *"God is my Judge"*	Belteshazzar: *"Bel protects his life"*
Hananiah: *"Yahweh is gracious"*	Shadrach: *"The command of Aku"*
Mishael: *"Who is what God is?"*	Meshack: *"Who is what Aku is?"*
Azariah: *"Yahweh is my Helper"*	Abed-Nego: *"Servant of Nebo"*

Yikes! Babylonian culture sought to remake these young men in its own image. But remember what Proverbs 23:7 tells us... *As a man thinks within his heart, so is he.* The labels of others didn't hold a candle to what God said of these men, and what they believed in their heart.

When I was young, my family moved to Moulton, Alabama, and we purchased a home right in the center of a cattle ranch. I would play cowboy every day! One thing my dad loved about our home was that the purchase of the house immediately secured his ability to one day establish ownership of the entire spread.

In the same way, the spirit of Babylon doesn't ask for control of everything at first—it just wants that center acre of your heart. Once it holds that part of you, it has access to all the rest of you. And that's why it has such an effect on your identity.

Zig Ziglar said this: *"It is impossible to perform consistently in a way that is inconsistent with how you see yourself."* [23]

Has someone ever tried to put a label on you? It might be an attractive label you want to cultivate, or it could be an offensive label you want to shed. Labels seek to control us and that's why it's crucial to first and foremost discover what God himself, our Maker, says about who we are.

Let's read on...

> [9] And God gave Daniel favor and compassion in the sight of the chief of the eunuchs, [10] and the chief of the eunuchs said to Daniel...

Here we meet this chief of the eunuchs who is in charge of Daniel and his friends. What does that make them? Eunuchs were men who were emasculated so that they could serve the king's wives without the king having to worry about anything sexual happening between them. There is something about the spirit of

Babylon that wants to rob a young man of his manhood. Or worse, get him to pervert it.

A biblical view of gender roles is ground zero for Babylon University. If God made you a young man, find a biblical role model for manhood and become what God made you to be. If God made you a young lady, find a biblical role model and become what God created you to be. And remember—sex is something to be kept for a husband and a wife to enjoy in the context of marriage. Don't give an inch on that. Hold your ground and wait for a partner who is seeking to do the same.

Thirdly, in Babylon, you're going to need to guard your Christian convictions…

> 8 But Daniel resolved that he would not defile himself with the king's food, or with the wine that he drank. Therefore he asked the chief of the eunuchs to allow him not to defile himself.

What difference did it make if he ate the king's meat? Well most theologians believe this meat had been ceremonially sacrificed to demonic idols, and to eat the meat was a similar ritual as when we take communion. It was an act of worship to pagan deities. Now think about it: Daniel had already cooperated on several other issues such as changing his name, the education process, and the way he dressed… but something about this meat bothered his conscience enough for him to refuse. And that's how it goes in our Babylon. There will be some things that you will be able to accept as you deal with the spirit of Babylon, but there will be other compromises that will penetrate your heart and compel you to take a stand.

I heard a story about a young man who had maintained a very high GPA all through college and was looking into medical school. He was asked by the board of one particular school, *"Will you perform an abortion if asked to do so?"* He said, *"No I will not. I'm not going to picket and protest, but I am a Christian and I am not comfortable doing so.*" They asked, "*What if that keeps you from getting into this institution?*" He replied, "*I don't have to get into this school, but I do have to honor my God.*" He didn't get in to that school but studied elsewhere and is known today as one of the top surgeons in Dallas.

Sometimes, following your convictions means missing out on opportunities. The world goes left, and you simply must go right. At other times, you'll have the chance to simply show the world around you a better way—God's way.

See how Daniel gets creative in following his convictions in verses 10–13:

> **10** "I fear my lord the king, who assigned your food and your drink; for why should he see that you were in worse condition than the youths who are of your own age? So you would endanger my head with the king." **11** Then Daniel said to the steward whom the chief of the eunuchs had assigned over Daniel, Hananiah, Mishael, and Azariah, **12** "Test your servants for ten days; let us be given vegetables to eat and water to drink. **13** Then let our appearance and the appearance of the youths who eat the king's food be observed by you, and deal with your servants according to what you see."

Notice Daniel's attitude in this passage. He wasn't obstinate or rebellious; he simply offered a creative alternative and trusted God for the results.

> **14** So he listened to them in this matter, and tested them for ten days. **15** At the end of ten days it was seen that they were better in appearance and fatter in flesh than all the youths who ate the king's food. **16** So the steward took away their food and the wine they were to drink, and gave them vegetables. **17** As for these four youths, God gave them learning and skill in all literature and wisdom, and Daniel had understanding in all visions

and dreams. [18] At the end of the time, when the king had commanded that they should be brought in, the chief of the eunuchs brought them in before Nebuchadnezzar. [19] And the king spoke with them, and among all of them none was found like Daniel, Hananiah, Mishael, and Azariah. Therefore they stood before the king. [20] And in every matter of wisdom and understanding about which the king inquired of them, he found them ten times better than all the magicians and enchanters that were in all his kingdom. [21] And Daniel was there until the first year of King Cyrus.

King Cyrus of Persia overthrew Babylon in 539 B.C. This means Daniel stood his ground for truth and boldly lived out his faith in a hostile culture for approximately 70 years! But Daniel was not simply a contrast to Babylonian culture; he was also a beacon of hope, just like God's people are today.

Andy Crouch said it this way:

> *"The exile is also a sign of hope. God's people are placed in the midst of*
> *the religion-assimilating, privilege-seeking, royal-food-serving, power-serving, name-changing kingdoms of the world to bear witness to those kingdoms that they are not the last word. They are placed there because God loves the world, including Babylon, and wants his ways to be known everywhere, not just within a religious enclave."[24]*

Daniel went about life in his Babylon with courage and conviction, and as a result, there is a man in heaven today named Nebuchadnezzar. But a much greater man than Daniel has come into another Babylon. Our Lord came into this world that hated Him to the point of crucifying Him, and because He willingly chose to walk that road, you and I are in the Kingdom of God. If you walk into your Babylon like Daniel, and like Jesus—you'll impact God's Kingdom like never before.

Questions to consider:

1. Do you have a "tribe" of like-minded believers around you? How do those relationships give you strength when you're faced with temptation or the cares of this world? Is there someone today who needs you to stand up next to them?

2. What labels or names you've been given have shaped your identity? Did you give yourself that label or did it come from someone else? How can the truth of what God says about you in His Word speak into that identity?

3. What is one conviction you refuse to compromise, no matter what happens in your Babylon? How do you decide what is okay and not okay when it comes to giving in to society's standards?

4. Do you believe that God has placed you in this culture during this season for a purpose? Take some time to ask Him today what He wants you to do as you stand for truth in your Babylon.

CHAPTER TEN

PICK A TEAM: WHO WILL YOU WORSHIP?

Identifying Your Idols and Laying Them Down for Good

I remember it like it was yesterday. There I was in middle school, standing outside with a group of kids waiting to be picked for a team. It was a nail-biting traumatizing experience! I get anxious just thinking about it, but do you know who was never anxious in those moments? The captains! They had total control. They knew who they wanted, and they could pick their teams as they wished. In many ways, you have the same choice today. You decide what team you play for and who you want to lock arms with in life. But you can't have it both ways. You have to pick a team. You have to choose whom you will worship.

It was Martin Luther who accurately observed: *The default setting of the human heart is to worship.*

He's right! In fact, psychologists call this the "religious instinct." As sociologist Talcott Parsons explained,

> *"There is no known human society without something which modern social scientist would classify as religion."*[25]

If you took a tribe of tiny humans from their mother's wombs, separated them from all outside influence and simply observed their development, you would discover that they have an innate desire to worship. Why? Because worship is something God hard wired into the human heart.

In Matthew 22:35–40 (NASB1995), someone asks Jesus a telling question.

> [35] One of them, a lawyer, asked Him a question, testing Him, [36] "Teacher, which is the great commandment in the Law?"
>
> [37] And He said to him, 'You shall love the Lord your God with all your heart, and with all your soul, and with all your mind.' [38] This is the great and foremost commandment.

This passage is all about worship. To love the one true God is to worship Him and Him alone. This is what you and I were created for—and it's in obedience to this the greatest commandment that we find our greatest joy and fulfillment. Logically then, to refuse to worship the one true God, or to worship something in His place, must be the greatest sin.

Now, the term *worship* is derived from the Old English word meaning, "worth-ship." It is an attribution of worth or value. We commonly speak of worship in conjunction with the word, *praise*. This is also where we get our word *appraisal*, which means "to attribute value to something." So we show our devotion, value, or love for God through worship. We value Him, His Word, and His presence above all else.

Now, if worship of the one true God lies at the very heart of what it means to be human—if it leads to our greatest joy and fulfillment in life—then you can bet that one of Satan's primary goals is to misdirect our worship from God to idols. Think about it, Satan can't make you stop worshipping. You're hardwired to do so! Therefore, he has to redirect your worship onto something else, something less. His desire is for you to love, value, and worship anything but God, thus breaking the greatest command, and thereby committing the greatest sin. And to be clear, this greatest sin is called "idolatry." One of the most repeated commands in the

Old Testament is this, *"Have no other gods before me."* Simply put, God forbids idolatry.

Take Adam in the garden as an example. Satan tempted him to value the word of the serpent over the word of God. You see, idolatry isn't always bowing down to a statue, but it is allowing something in your life to take a place of greater prominence than God.

In 1 Corinthians 10:19–20, Paul reveals that behind every idol there is a demon. He means an actual individual being, a fallen angel who serves Satan. Demons are willing to work through anyone or anything in order to misdirect your worship. Be assured that any time you are willing to obey someone or something above Christ, you are being seduced by the enemy and you are a practicing idolater.

Colossians 3:5 (NASB1995) says this:

> 5 Therefore consider the members of your earthly body as dead to immorality, impurity, passion, evil desire, and greed, which amounts to idolatry.

Here's a hard truth: God's Word tells you to wait to have sex until marriage, but your boyfriend says, *"If you loved me, you would."* If you obey your boyfriend rather than God, you are committing idolatry and worshipping your boyfriend.

Consider the many gods worshipped in the Greco-Roman world:

- Venus, the goddess of lust and physical immorality
- Ploutos, the god of wealth
- Bacchus, the god of drunkenness
- Apollo, the god of music
- Fama, the goddess of fame
- Juventas, the goddess of youth

Before you think these gods were harmless myths, understand that they were in fact demons who hid behind idols and sought to misdirect worship. And guess what? Not much has changed. The names and methods may have shifted, but Venus still seeks to lure humanity into valuing sex more than Christ. Ploutos still tempts people the world over to worship wealth more than God.

The question remains the same... who will you worship?

Real or Counterfeit?

All idolatry follows the same pattern. It involves a counterfeit god, a counterfeit preacher, a counterfeit church, and a counterfeit hell. You see this structure played out in Daniel 3:1–30.

Verse 1 says,

> [1] King Nebuchadnezzar made an image of gold, whose height was sixty cubits and its breadth six cubits. He set it up on the plain of Dura, in the province of Babylon.

You're probably not up to speed on your ancient measurements so let me explain. Nebuchadnezzar built an idol that was ninety feet tall and ninety feet wide—about three times higher than an average church building. Unlike most church buildings, however, Nebuchadnezzar made the image entirely of gold. Why is that significant? Do you recall the earlier episode in Daniel chapter 2 when God gave Nebuchadnezzar a dream where He foretold that an inferior kingdom would one day rule over Babylon? Rather than honor the decree of God, Nebuchadnezzar seems to say, "*We will see about that.*" And he makes another statue that competes with the revelation of God. And it's not partly gold, it's entirely gold.

But where did all of that gold come from? It likely came from the temple of God in Jerusalem. Can you imagine how insulting that would be for those Hebrew young men? Gold from God's holy temple was being formed into a graven image. It's as if he was shouting from the rooftops, "*I Nebuchadnezzar will be the eternal king, not Christ, the stone from heaven.*"

Not only does this passage include a counterfeit god, it also has a counterfeit preacher.

> 4 And the herald proclaimed aloud, "You are commanded, O peoples, nations, and languages…"

It may sound extreme, but it's true. Satan calls and equips counterfeit pastors and evangelists to champion the cause of his idol. The word *herald* in this verse is the same word for what I do every week: I "declare the message of the King." I have no right to modify the message or tweak it to make it sound more appealing… I am to herald the truth and proclaim it.

Thirdly, this passage reveals a counterfeit church…

> 4 And the herald proclaimed aloud, "You are commanded, O peoples, nations, and languages…"

The church is a mixed multitude of every tribe and tongue worshipping and serving the one true God. But Satan continually produces a counterfeit church. Ironically, many scholars believe that this story in Daniel took place on the same plain as the location of the Tower of Babel. Remember that sordid tale? God told the people of earth to fill the land and multiply, but they didn't want to, so they built a tower instead. They elevated their agenda over God's, worshipping themselves above him. And it seems like this statue is seeking to do the same thing.

Keep reading in verse 5:

> 5 "… that when you hear the sound of the horn, pipe, lyre, trigon, harp, bagpipe, and every kind of music, you are to fall down and worship the golden image that King Nebuchadnezzar has set up."

You've got the idol. You've got the preacher. You've got the congregation. And now you've got the worship music. It's an abhorrent church service for a counterfeit god.

Imagine in your mind's eye a ninety-foot statue covered in gold, standing in the blazing bright Middle Eastern sun. Then the plains erupt with a cacophony of music, filling the region. And from all across the land, people responded by bowing down to express their reverence and worship.

And finally, Daniel 3 shows us a counterfeit hell…

> [6] "And whoever does not fall down and worship shall immediately be cast into a burning fiery furnace."

Now, you may be thinking that such a dramatic expression of pagan worship has nothing to do with our lives today. But remember what Paul wrote in 1 Corinthians 10:11…

> [11] Now these things happened to them as an example, but they were written down for our instruction, on whom the end of the ages has come.

This story in Daniel actually happened, but one of the reasons it happened was so we could draw modern-day correlations to these experiences. In what way does this ninety-foot statue compare to the idols you will face in your daily life?

Consider these questions when pondering idols in your own life…

- Am I tempted to obey this person or thing over Jesus?
- Am I listening to the word of this person or thing faithfully, regularly, and with the sort of allegiance I owe to the one true God?
- Am I regularly having to miss the gathering of the saints in order to give my time to this person or thing?
- Do I find myself expressing worth or worship to this person or thing that belongs only to my Creator?
- Do I fear the punishment of this person or thing if I do not comply?

Take for example the demonic idol of popularity:

> A person who worships popularity might find the one supremely popular person and take his or her advice as to how they should act or think. This is their pastor.
>
> They may choose to miss time with God's people if the popular crowd has competing plans. This is their church.
>
> They will erupt with passionate zeal seldom seen amongst the most devoted Christians if they can't buy the right clothes or join the right activities to remain in the popular crowd. Why? Because they don't want to suffer the wrath of their counterfeit god and be cast out. This is their hell.

Let's see what happens next in Daniel chapter 3, when the Chaldeans rat on the Jews…

> [12] There are certain Jews whom you have appointed over the affairs of the province of Babylon: Shadrach, Meshach, and Abednego. These men, O king, pay no attention to you; they do not serve your gods or worship the golden image that you have set up."

Nothing will make you stand out more than the simple fact that you don't worship the cultural idols everyone else bows down to.

I remember well the days of preaching at student camps and conferences. These kids would get so fired up that they were ready to charge hell with a water pistol. Some dynamic student pastor would gather them around a campfire and tell them to find a twig to symbolize their old life. Then all at once, we would throw our twigs in the fire. But hear this: Christian commitment is not found in tossing a twig into a campfire. Instead, it manifests itself when someone hears an inappropriate joke in the lunchroom and leaves the table because they are tired of the foolishness.

So often, Christian commitment is found in what you won't do. The early church didn't suffer for worshipping Jesus, they suffered for *not* worshipping Caesar.

Revealing Your Idols

^{13} Then Nebuchadnezzar in furious rage…

Sometimes, the best indication that you are worshipping a demonic idol is undue anger when someone offends your idol. What do you get unreasonably upset about? Chances are, that's your idol.

> ^{13} Then Nebuchadnezzar in furious rage commanded that Shadrach, Meshach, and Abednego be brought. So they brought these men before the king. ^{14} Nebuchadnezzar answered and said to them, "Is it true, O Shadrach, Meshach, and Abednego, that you do not serve my gods or worship the golden image that I have set up?…"

> ^{16} Shadrach, Meshach, and Abednego answered and said to the king, "O Nebuchadnezzar, we have no need to answer you in this matter. ^{17} If this be so, our God whom we serve is able to deliver us from the burning fiery furnace, and he will deliver us out of your hand, O king. ^{18} But if not, be it known to you, O king, that we will not serve your gods or worship the golden image that you have set up."

These men knew the power of God, they just didn't know the plan of God. Many times we believe that God can deliver us, we just don't know *if* He will. And that's just the way it is. God does not always tell us plans, nor does He have to, but you can always know God's heart!

Do you know what else reveals your idols? The things you pray for. Sometimes you ask God to give you more of your idol. If He doesn't, you're angry inside because He doesn't worship the same idol you do. When these Hebrews expressed their belief that

God could save them from the fire but didn't have to, they were showing that they trusted in the power of their God even though they did not know His plan. They were refusing to substitute their God for the idol of comfort.

> [19] Then Nebuchadnezzar was filled with fury, and the expression of his face was changed against Shadrach, Meshach, and Abednego. He ordered the furnace heated seven times more than it was usually heated.

> [20] And he ordered some of the mighty men of his army to bind Shadrach, Meshach, and Abednego, and to cast them into the burning fiery furnace. [21] Then these men were bound in their cloaks, their tunics, their hats, and their other garments, and they were thrown into the burning fiery furnace. [22] Because the king's order was urgent and the furnace overheated, the flame of the fire killed those men who took up Shadrach, Meshach, and Abednego. [23] And these three men, Shadrach, Meshach, and Abednego, fell bound into the burning fiery furnace. [24] Then King Nebuchadnezzar was astonished and rose up in haste. He declared to his counselors, "Did we not cast three men bound into the fire?" They answered and said to the king, "True, O king." [25] He answered and said, "But I see four men unbound, walking in the midst of the fire, and they are not hurt; and the appearance of the fourth is like a son of the gods."

Our God has a flair for the dramatic! When it looks like it's all over... *behold there stands a fourth man, one like unto the Son of God...*

Don't miss this truth: It is the common practice of the Almighty not to intervene until your conviction has been placed on full display.

The year 2012 was a rough one for me. Our senior adult

pastor died suddenly, our student pastor was called to another church, and our worship pastor lost his ministry and family over immorality, all in the same year. Not to mention, my father became sick and had to move in with our family. In the midst of it all, there was a tremendous theological argument taking place in our church, and although it was keeping with our statement of faith, it was a sore spot for some of our members.

There was a defining moment in which I felt like everything was falling apart. I remember walking out to my backyard one Friday night and saying, *"God if you can hear me, and if I'm on the right track, would you give me some sort of a sign?"* I had never asked for a sign before that night, and I haven't asked for one since. But that night I just needed one. I stayed out there for a long time... but nothing happened.

I walked in and told my wife what I had asked of God, and how nothing had happened. She said, *"What are you going to do?"* I said, *"All I know to do is preach the Word."* So, I woke up that Sunday, mad at God, disappointed in my circumstances, and confused. But I made the decision to pack up my notes, drive to church, and preach the truth of God's Word, regardless of my feelings. I was literally a mile and a half from the church when I heard a text come through on my phone. I could tell it was a very long text message and I felt compelled to pull over and read it. The text was from one of the deacons in our church.

Now to preface this part of the story, some people are more "charismatic" than others. They receive a word from God about every 10 minutes! But this man was about as charismatic as a rock. That's why his message impacted me so deeply. He shared with me that on Friday night, around the time when I was praying in my backyard, God woke him up. He said his room was filled with light and he saw some words written on his wall, *"Follow Zach, he is following Jesus."* He said, *"Pastor, I sat up and prayed for you all night.... I just want you to know that I've got your back."*

Now think of the wisdom in how God spoke peace to me. He didn't want me to live by a sign or wonder, He wanted me to live by conviction. But in His kindness, He also taught me that creating a sign was just as easy for Him!

Charles Spurgeon says it best: *"Beloved, you must go into the furnace if you are to have the nearest and dearest dealings with Christ Jesus."*[26]

I am praying for you, whoever you are, wherever you are. I'm asking God to grant you the courage and conviction to face your blazing furnace with boldness and strength. I'm asking God to shed His light on the idols of your heart, and for Him to tear them down with the unshakable power of His love. May you experience His peace today as you worship Him and Him alone… whether in, or your eternal home.

Questions to consider:

1. Can you identify anyone or anything in your life that you might classify as an idol? What needs to go?

2. How does what God did for Shadrach, Meshach, and Abednego encourage you to resist bowing down to the idols of this world? Do you truly believe God is powerful enough to rescue you from the fire?

3. What will it take for God to be enough in your life? How can you draw close to him and experience his love for you in a more intimate way?

4. What steps can you take today to let go of the idolatry you have allowed to take root in your heart?

CONCLUSION

Where do we go from here?

Can we reclaim the ship of culture and once again drop our anchor into the Rock of Ages? If you have read this far and processed the claims I have made in this book, then perhaps we do stand a fighting chance.

If we are going to turn things around, we must be culture makers, not simply culture critics. Start with your family - create a culture in your home that your kids yearn to replicate. Here are a few simple pieces of advice that have served our family well:

1. **Family Meals -** At least once a week, we have a home-cooked family meal. We have a few simple rules:

   - **Everyone pitches in** - either in preparation or clean-up
   - **No devices at the table**
   - **One conversation at a time** - there are six people at our table: my wife, our three kids, and my mother. Someone typically has an issue they wish to discuss. Those conversations allow us to disciple and shape the worldview of our family.

2. **Family Worship -** On each Lord's Day, you will find us worshipping together in our local church. That has been our pattern for nearly 25 years, in the good times and the bad. I cannot overstate the importance of building your family around the ministry of a strong local church.

3. **Family Creativity** - Each person in our family is producing a cultural contribution of some sort. Some are more involved in political change, other's are engaged in the arts. Writing a book like this is a meager attempt to not only be a cultural critic but to add something to the equation.

Those are just a few of the things that have served to keep our family on course over the decades.

To change the world, you must change the nation,
To change the nation, you must change your state,
To change your state you must change your community,
To change your community, you must change your church,
To change your church - start with your family.

Zach Terry - Author

---

[1] Akops Balogh, "The Ancient Heresy Driving Modern Identity," *Current Events*, The Gospel Coalition (March 3, 2019), accessed May 31, 2024, https://au.thegospelcoalition.org/article/ancient-heresy-driving-modern-identity/.

[2] Adam Hayes, "Boomerang Children: Meaning, Impact, Around the World," Investopedia, (March 13, 2022), accessed May 31, 2024, https://www.investopedia.com/terms/b/boomerangs.asp.

[3] Karl Marx, "The Pale Maiden," in *A Book of Verse,* accessed 5/30/2024, https://www.marxists.org/archive/marx/works/1837-pre/verse/index.htm.

[4] Victor Davis Hanson, "Are Americans becoming Sovietized?" *Las Vegas Review Journal*, May 8, 2021. https://www.reviewjournal.com/opinion/opinion-columns/victor-davis-hanson/victor-davis-hanson-are-americans-becoming-sovietized-2349846/

[5] Henry Blackaby, "On The Brink of Crisis: A Call To Prayer" (Keynote Address, National Day of Prayer, Lancaster, PA, May 6, 2004).

[6] George Orwell, *1984* (London: Penguin Classics, 2021), 248.

[7] W. B. Yeats, 1865–1939, *The Collected Poems of W.B. Yeats* (New York: Macmillan, 1959), 187.

[8] Vance Havner, *Why Not Just Be Christians* (Shoals, IN: Kingsley Press, 2015), XX

[9] Andy Stanley, *Making Vision Stick* (Grand Rapids, MI: Zondervan, July 30, 2007), 277, Kindle.

[10] Kao-Ping Chua, MD, PhD; Anna Volerman, MD; Jason Zhang, BS; Joanna Hua, BS; Rena M. Conti, PhD, "Antidepressant Dispensing to US Adolescents and Young Adults: 2016–2022," *Pediatrics*, Volume 153, Issue 3 (March 2024) https://publications.aap.org/pediatrics/article/153/3/e2023064245/196655/Antidepressant-Dispensing-to-US-Adolescents-and?autologincheck=redirected.

[11] William Cowper, "God Moves in Mysterious Ways," (1774).

[12] Erika Edwards and Maggie Fox, "Teens Spend 'Astounding' Nine Hours a Day in Front of Screens: Researchers," NBC News, (November 3, 2015) https://www.nbcnews.com/health/kids-health/kids-spend-astounding-nine-hours-day-front-screens-researchers-n456446.

[13] Josh Howarth, "Internet Traffic from Mobile Devices," *Exploding Topics*, (July 2024) https://explodingtopics.com/blog/mobile-internet-traffic.

[14] Albert Mohler, Foreword in *God and the Transgender Debate* by Andrew T. Walker (Epsom, UK: The Good Book Company, 2022), 9.

[15] Daniel Sanderson, "Children to be allowed to change genders in Scottish schools," *The Telegraph*, (April 8, 2024), accessed May 31, 2024, https://www.telegraph.co.uk/news/2024/04/08/children-change-gender-scottish-schools-review/.

[16] Paul McHugh, "Transgender Surgery Isn't the Solution: A drastic physical change doesn't address underlying psycho-social troubles," Op-ed, *WSJ* (June 12, 2014).

[17] Ryan T. Anderson, "Sex Reassignment Doesn't Work. Here Is the Evidence.", *The Heritage Foundation* (March 9, 2018), accessed May 31, 2024, https://www.heritage.org/gender/commentary/sex-reassignment-doesnt-work-here-the-evidence.

[18] Craig Blomberg, "Matthew," Vol. 22, *The New American Commentary* (Nashville: Broadman & Holman Publishers, 1992), 289.

[19] David Finkelhor, Anne Shattuck, Heather A Turner, Sherry L Hamby, "The lifetime prevalence of child sexual abuse and sexual assault assessed in late adolescence," *Journal of Adolescent Health* Vol. 55, Issue 3 (February 26, 2014), accessed May 31, 2024, https://pubmed.ncbi.nlm.nih.gov/24582321/.

[20] Pliny, Natural History Book 35, Section 17 Translated by H.Rackham (1952), with some minor alterations.

[21] Petronius, The Satyricon of Petronius, Chapter Three, XVII.

[22] Christian Smith and Melina Lundquist Denton, *Soul Searching: The Religious and Spiritual Lives of American Teenagers* (New York: Oxford University Press, 2005), 162.

[23] Zig Ziglar, *Better Than Good: Creating a Life You Can't Wait to Live* (Nashville: Thomas Nelson, 2007), XX.

[24] Andy Crouch, quoted in "Making the Most of College," Blog, Chesterton House (August 7, 2007), https://chestertonhouse.org/blog/making-most-

college/.

[25] Talcott Parsons in the Introduction to Max Weber, *The Sociology of Religion* (London: Methuen & Co Ltd, 1965), xxvii.

[26] Charles Haddon Spurgeon, "Consolation in the Furnace," Sermon, Metropolitan Tabernacle Pulpit, Vol. 11 (November 26, 1865).

ABOUT THE AUTHOR

Zachary C Terry

Pastor Zach Terry
President and Lead Teach of Maximum Life
Zach, a devoted family man, is married to Julie and they are blessed with three children. They reside in North Florida, where Zach fulfills his role as the Senior Pastor of the First Baptist Church of Fernandina Beach, FL.

Pastor Zach's voice can be heard faithfully teaching the truth on terrestrial radio to a potential audience of 3 million listeners throughout the Southern United States. He is the author of Our Fight: Survive and Thrive in Spiritual Warfare and has been featured as a contributor in the Alabama Baptist Newspaper, Lifeway's Stewardship Podcast, the Florida, and the Baptist Foundation Podcast.

ACADEMIC:
Pastor Zach's commitment to his faith is evident in his academic pursuits. He holds a Master's degree from the prestigious Southern Baptist Theological Seminary, where he was honored with the Westminster John Knox Press Award for e xcellence in preaching and teaching the Christian scriptures. He is furthering his education by pursuing a Doctorate Degree in Leadership from the same institution.

INTERNATIONAL:
Zach invests considerable time with Pastors, training them for more effective service. He has spoken internationally in Honduras, Guatemala, and Belize at Pastor's conferences. In 2018, he was invited by the National Police Force of Honduras to speak to all active duty officers on the subject of biblical manhood. A subsequent invitation was given to return to Honduras to address the entire student body of the National Police Academy. In 2019, he met with the President and First Lady of Guatemala, the Florida Baptist's One More Child, to help end child trafficking. Soon, he will travel to Peru to help forward the work of One More Child in that country.

LEADERSHIP:
Pastor Zach has served on the Florida Baptist State Board of Missions Administrative Committee. He's part of the exclusive "Large Church Roundtable," where thriving Pastors gather annually to encourage one another and to strategize for the future.

Zach has been invited to give the invocation for numerous sporting events like the Daytona Motor Speedway, home to the Daytona 500, and has spoken at the Lucas Oil Racing series.

In 2020, Vice President Mike Pence invited Pastor Zach to the White House to work with a group of Christian leaders to further religious freedom throughout the United States. In 2022, Pastor Zach stood at the lectern of the Florida Senate to pray over the state leaders for their opening session. In 2024, he was privileged to open a session of the Congress of the United States in prayer.

BOOKS BY THIS AUTHOR

Our Fight

The spiritual battlefield is scattered with wounded soldiers. Homes are ablaze and under attack. Yet we are told that our weapons are mighty to the point that we not only can survive the attack, but counter attack and take new ground. "Our Fight" is a field manual for the solider of Christ's Kingdom. It helps to identify your enemy as well as explains tactics for bringing about his ultimate defeat.